TIMESAVER FOR EXA

IELTS Writing

(4.0–5.5)

By Jon Marks

■■SCHOLASTIC

Contents

Introduction

Who is this book for?

This book is for teachers of students preparing for the Academic version of the IELTS test, and who are aiming for a score of 4.0–5.5. It is an ideal supplement to any IELTS preparation coursebook, especially for those new to the exam. The topics and activities reflect those typical of the IELTS Academic test and are designed especially to appeal to young adults. This resource is also suitable for use with any intermediate classes who wish to begin to develop their academic writing, especially with a view to academic study.

The IELTS test: an overview

The International English Language Testing System (IELTS) is a test that measures the language proficiency of people who want to study or work in environments where English is used as a language of communication. An easy-to-use 9-band scale clearly identifies proficiency level, from non-user (band score 1) through to expert (band score 9).

IELTS is available in two test formats – Academic or General Training – and provides a valid and accurate assessment of the four language skills: listening, reading, writing and speaking. This Timesaver title focuses on the Academic version of the test.

There are four components to the test.

Reading 60 minutes. There are three texts with 40 questions.

Writing 60 minutes. There are two writing Tasks. Task 1 has a minimum of 150 words. Task 2 has a minimum of 250 words.

Listening approximately 30 minutes (plus 10 minutes for transferring answers). There are four sections with 40 questions.

Speaking 11–14 minutes. There are three parts.

Scoring

Each component of the test is given a band score. The average of the four scores produces the overall band score. You do not pass or fail IELTS; you receive a score.

The IELTS scale

Band score	Skill level	Description
9	Expert user	The test taker has fully operational command of the language. Their use of English is appropriate, accurate and fluent, and shows complete understanding.
8	Very good user	The test taker has fully operational command of the language with only occasional unsystematic inaccuracies and inappropriate usage. They may misunderstand some things in unfamiliar situations. They handle complex and detailed argumentation well.
7	Good user	The test taker has operational command of the language, though with occasional inaccuracies, inappropriate usage and misunderstandings in some situations. They generally handle complex language well and understand detailed reasoning.
6	Competent user	The test taker has an effective command of the language despite some inaccuracies, inappropriate usage and misunderstandings. They can use and understand fairly complex language, particularly in familiar situations.
5	Modest user	The test taker has a partial command of the language and copes with overall meaning in most situations, although they are likely to make many mistakes. They should be able to handle basic communication in their own field.
4	Limited user	The test taker's basic competence is limited to familiar situations. They frequently show problems in understanding and expression. They are not able to use complex language.
3	Extremely limited user	The test taker conveys and understands only general meaning in very familiar situations. There are frequent breakdowns in communication.
2	Intermittent user	The test taker has great difficulty understanding spoken and written English.
1	Non-user	The test taker has no ability to use the language except a few isolated words.

For full details on the IELTS test, go to: www.ielts.org

How do I use this book?

The book is divided into 12 pairs of lessons and one final review lesson. The first lesson in each pair covers Task 1 and the second Task 2 of the IELTS academic writing component. Both lessons are based around a theme which IELTS candidates are currently required to write about. Use the lessons to supplement your coursebook by providing extra practice of particular parts of the test or topic areas. The activities also provide thorough practice of exam skills.

- The activities are designed to be teacher-led but are used without separate Teacher's notes. Clear instructions are on the pages, which are all photocopiable.

- The test section, question type and lesson focus are clearly labelled in each lesson.

- The lessons have been designed to cover one hour of class time, depending on class size and language level.

- The comprehensive answer key at the back of the book provides an explanation of the answers. It also provides example answers for each of the **EXAM TASKS** and the test questions.

- There are writing tips in each lesson to raise students' awareness of the most important strategies for academic writing.

- Some activities ask students to work in pairs or groups to maximise their engagement with the writing skills and language. These can be adapted depending on context and class size.

- There is an **EXAM TASK** in every lesson, which requires students to write a complete essay. These Tasks are ideal to set as homework, or as timed writing practice under exam conditions in class.

How important are academic Writing skills for exam success?

The IELTS test requires candidates to be able to use a wide range of writing skills. In Task 1, candidates may be required to describe data presented in one or more graphs, charts or tables. Alternatively, they may have to describe a diagram of a machine, a device or a process and be asked to explain how it works. They may also be required to describe a map and to either evaluate the suitability of two possible development sites or to describe changes that have occurred in a place over time.

Candidates will need to demonstrate an ability to identify the most important and relevant information in a graph, chart, table, map or diagram and to organise their answer well, using language accurately in an academic style. In Task 2, candidates are asked to write a discursive essay about a given topic and are required to write a response which is fully relevant to the specific question set. This task evaluates the candidate's ability to present a clear argument, which is relevant and well-organised.

The activities in this book introduce candidates to each of the Task 1 and Task 2 question types in turn and provide tips on structuring answers logically as well as on avoiding common pitfalls. Example answers are also provided for candidates to analyse and to use as a guide. There is also an example answer for each of the **EXAM TASKS** in the Answer Key at the back of the book.

To achieve a score of 4.0 to 5.5 in the IELTS Writing test, candidates need to organise ideas into an appropriate structure, and they need to write in a style which is appropriate for answering an exam question. They need to use vocabulary which is relevant to the topic and accurate for making their intended points, and they need to use suitable grammar to convey concepts accurately and to link ideas, though, at this level, they are not expected to use complex grammatical structures accurately. The lessons in this book offer extensive guidance and practice opportunities for structuring answers and for writing in an appropriate style. The lessons also practise useful vocabulary connected with popular IELTS topics, and practise grammar which is useful for various basic functions in academic writing, such as describing trends or expressing cause and effect relationships.

The Timesaver series

The Timesaver series provides hundreds of ready-made lessons for all language levels and age groups, covering skills work, language practice and cross-curricular and cross-cultural material. See the full range of print and digital resources at: **www.scholastic.co.uk/elt**

Getting started

1 **Work in pairs. Answer the questions.**

a) What kind of writing can you see in the photos? Which kind of writing do you do most?

b) What other types of writing do people do?

c) Do you need to write a lot in your everyday life? What kinds of things do you write?

d) Do you always need to write in full sentences or use correct punctuation?

e) In the IELTS Writing test, do you need to use full sentences and good punctuation? Why?

Exam tip

In the IELTS Writing test, you need to put your ideas into full sentences. These sentences must have correct punctuation. You must do this to get a good mark.

How many of the following can you find in this tip box?

- sentences ....4...........
- capital letters ....
- full stops ....
- commas ....
- question marks ....

2 **Match the sentence beginnings (1–5) and endings (a–e).**

1) We use sentences
2) We use capital letters
3) We use full stops
4) We use commas
5) We use question marks

a) to start a sentence.
b) to end a sentence (if it is a question).
c) to give one complete idea.
d) to end a sentence (if it isn't a question).
e) to separate ideas in a sentence or items in a list.

3a **Work in pairs. What do you know about Task 1 of the IELTS Writing test?**

a) What do you have to write about?   b) How many words must you write?   c) How much time do you have?

3b **Read the information below and check your answers. Then rewrite the information with correct punctuation.**

a) in the IELTS Writing test, you will see a picture (a diagram, a graph or a table). You need to describe the data in the picture You have to report the important information, You do not need to give an opinion?

....

....

....

b) you have to write at least 150 words you can write more than this, but you must not write less than this.

....

....

c) you only have about 20 minutes to understand the picture and write your description you cannot afford to waste any time

....

....

4a Work in pairs. Look at the diagram. Choose the best summary.

A The diagram explains what kind of people like pots.

B The diagram explains how pots are made.

C The diagram explains how many pots are made every year

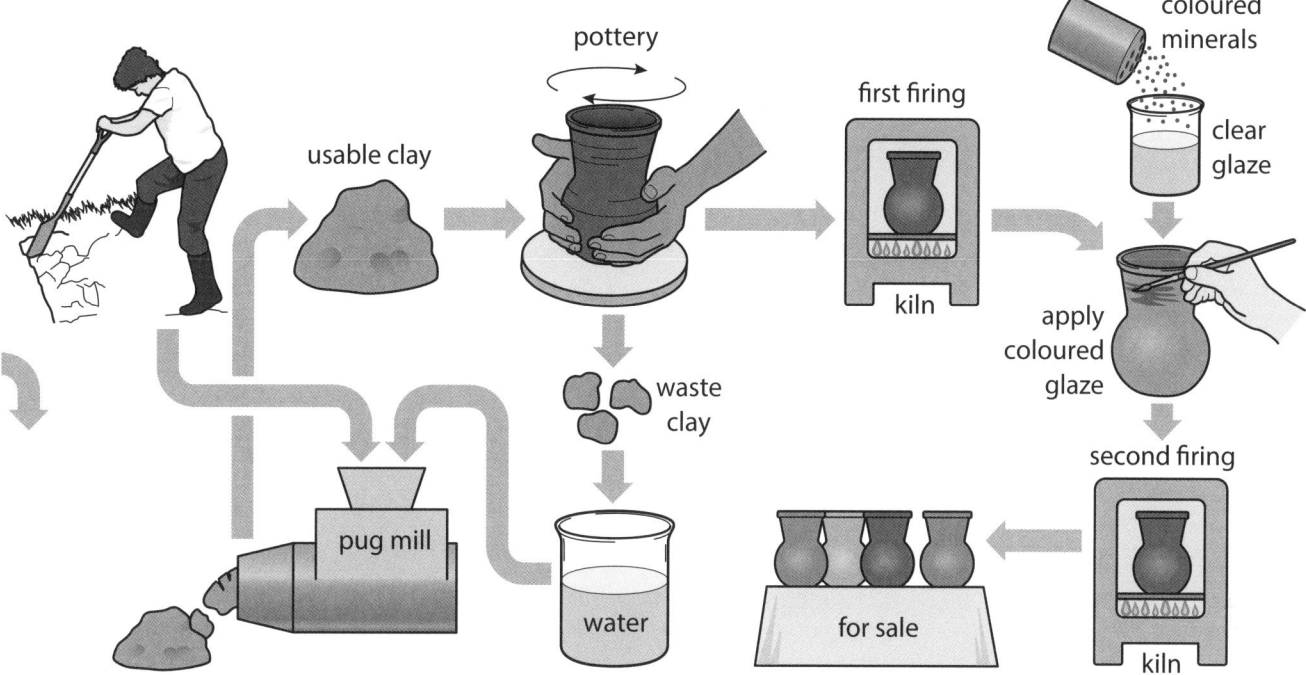

4b Use the pictures to help you guess what the words in the diagram mean. Match the words in the box with the definitions (a–i).

> clay   firing   glaze   ~~kiln~~   minerals   pot   pottery   pug mill   waste

a) a hot oven ...._kiln_........

b) a container, which you can put things in (e.g. food or drink) ....

c) the material we make pots from ....

d) the process of making something hard by adding heat ....

e) something which makes a pot shiny and attractive ....

f) what you don't need or want ....

g) chemical substances ....

h) a place where people make pots ....

i) a machine which mixes pieces of clay to make it usable (easy to use) ....

> **Exam tip**
>
> In IELTS Writing Task 1, there may be some words you don't know in the diagram. Use the pictures to help you understand the words.

5a Read the introduction about the diagram. Rewrite it into two sentences. Add full stops and capital letters.

this diagram shows the process of making handmade pots from clay, starting with digging the clay out of the ground it also shows how we can use waste clay, and how we can make coloured glaze

....

....

5b **What is the purpose of the introduction in exercise 5a? Choose the correct answer.**

    A to give an overview of what we can see in the diagram

    B to explain in detail what is happening

    C to give an opinion about making pots

6 **Work in pairs. Look at two more introductions about the diagram. Why are they not good introductions?**

    a) *Many people enjoy making pots by hand. In my country, this has been a tradition for thousands of years. In this essay, I would like to discuss why people still use this method.*

    b) *First, you need some clay. This is important because without clay, you can't make anything.*

7a **Here is a list of points to include in a description of the diagram. Complete the points with words from the diagram.**

    a) someone digs ....*clay*........ from the ground

    b) the pieces of clay go into a .... , so that it can be usable

    c) usable clay goes to a .... and someone makes it into pots

    d) .... clay from this process goes into water

    e) waste clay also goes back to the .... , which turns it back into usable clay

    f) the pot goes into a .... for the first firing

    g) someone applies coloured .... to the pot

    h) you can make glaze by mixing coloured .... with clear glaze

    i) the pots return to the kiln for the second ....

7b **Look at part of a description. What do the words in bold do? Choose the correct answer.**

    __First__, someone digs the clay from the ground. __Next__, the pieces of clay go into a pug mill, so that it can be usable. __After that__, the usable clay goes into a pottery, and someone makes it into pots.

    A they give extra information about the process

    B they explain what words like *clay* or *pug mill* mean

    C they show how one thing in the process happens after another thing

8 **Write a description of the diagram in exercise 4a. Use the ideas in exercise 7a and the words in exercise 7b. Check your work for punctuation (capital letters and full stops).**

EXAM TASK: Writing (Task 1)

The diagram shows how pots are made by hand.

Summarise the information by selecting and reporting the main features and make comparisons where relevant.

Write at least 150 words.

What's the topic?

1 **Work in pairs. Discuss the questions.**

a) What kinds of things do you use the internet for?

b) How much time a day do you spend using the internet?

c) Do you think people spend too much time on the internet?

d) Look at the photos. What are some of the advantages and disadvantages of using the internet?

2a **Work in pairs. What do you know about Task 2 of the IELTS Writing test?**

a) What do you have to write about?

b) How many words must you write, and how much time do you have for this?

2b **Read the information below and check your answers. Then complete the information with words from the box.**

60   250   ~~essay~~   opinion   question

In Task 2 of the IELTS Writing test, candidates have to write an **(1)** _essay_ . You will have a **(2)** _____ which will ask you to discuss or argue different points of view (for example, the advantages and disadvantages of something), and give your **(3)** _____ about something.

For this part of the Writing test, you will need to write at least **(4)** _____ words. You must follow the instructions given in the question, and you need to write in an academic style. The complete IELTS Writing test (Task 1 and Task 2) lasts **(5)** _____ minutes, and you should spend around 40 minutes of this on Task 2.

3 **The information in exercise 2b is written in two paragraphs. Choose the correct answers.**

a) We sometimes / always need to organise essays into paragraphs.

b) A paragraph is made of one / more than one sentence.

c) There is / isn't a space between each paragraph.

d) A paragraph has one clear topic / lots of different topics.

e) The first / last sentence of the paragraph usually explains what its topic is.

4 **Work in pairs. Look at the Task 2 question. What is your opinion?**

People spend too much time using the internet and not enough time talking with family, friends and neighbours. Do you agree or disagree with this opinion?

Exam tip

In IELTS Writing Task 2, you need to write in paragraphs to get a good mark. Paragraphs help the reader understand what your main topics are, and what you want to discuss in your essay.

5 **Look at the essay. Match the topics (a–e) with the paragraphs (1–4).**

a) agreeing with the opinion in the question ....*2*....

b) summarising the essay, and mostly disagreeing with the opinion in the question ....

c) disagreeing with the opinion in the question ....

d) introducing the essay and the things that the writer wants to discuss ....

1 *Many people spend several hours each day using the internet. **In this essay, I will** discuss whether I agree that this stops people from spending enough time with their family, friends and neighbours.*

2 *I agree that some people spend too much time online. **For example**, some people play games online, or use the internet for shopping or checking news. Many people spend too much time in front of screens, which can be unhealthy. It means that they do not communicate with real people, in the real world. It is true that people nowadays prefer looking at their smartphones to talking with their families, friends and neighbours.*

3 *However, the internet can also help people to communicate. Millions of people use it to make new friends or stay in contact with old ones. Family members who live far away from each other can communicate with each other any time they want to, thanks to new technology. I do not think that a conversation which uses text messages or video calls is very different to a face-to-face conversation. Many community groups use social media to help organise events and to get new members. **In my opinion**, people can communicate and make friends more easily than before the internet existed.*

4 ***In conclusion***, *I do not agree that using the internet means that people don't spend enough time talking to their families, friends and neighbours. I believe that it has increased the amount of communication between people, and offers new ways for people to communicate.*

Exam tip

Phrases like *In this essay, … , For example, … , In my opinion … ,* and *In conclusion, …* are useful for organising your ideas and making your essay clearer to read.

6a **Match the phrases in bold in exercise 5 to the reasons the writer uses them (a–d).**

a) to introduce a final paragraph *In conclusion* ....

b) to give his/her personal view ....

c) to explain something, by giving examples ....

d) to say what the essay will include ....

6b **Match the phrases (1–4) with phrases with a similar meaning (a–d).**

1) In this essay, I will …   a) For instance

2) In my opinion, …   b) To summarise

3) For example, …   c) I am going to …

4) In conclusion, …   d) I believe that …

7a Work in pairs or small groups. Look at the Task 2 question and the plan. Discuss ideas for paragraphs 2 and 3.

EXAM TASK: Writing (Task 2)

Some people think that old houses should be knocked down to build new houses or apartment blocks. Others think that old houses should be protected because they are part of a nation's history. Discuss both views and give your own opinion.

Give reasons for your answer and include any relevant examples from your knowledge or experience.

You should write at least 250 words.

1 Introduction paragraph	One or two sentences to introduce the topic, then a sentence starting: *In this essay, I will discuss …*
2 Reasons to knock down old houses	
3 Reasons to protect old houses	
4 Conclusion paragraph	Your opinion, starting: *In conclusion, …*

7b Work with another pair or group. Listen to other students' ideas. Decide what your own opinion is: do you think that old houses should be knocked down or protected?

8 Write your essay in at least 250 words. Make sure you write in clear paragraphs.

Academic subjects

1a **Work in pairs. Discuss the questions about students in your country.**

a) What subjects have you studied at school?

b) Is there something you would like to study in the future?

c) What university subjects are most popular with students in your country?

d) Is it more common to find more men than women studying certain subjects?

e) Do you think everyone should study a foreign language in school?

1b **Write examples of academic subjects for these categories.**

- arts and humanities _history_

- social sciences

- sciences

- professional degrees

2 **Look at the Task 1 question and the chart. Choose the best overview of the data.**

> The chart shows the numbers of undergraduates studying arts, sciences, social sciences and professional training subjects at Torrington University in 1990 and 2010.
>
> Summarise the information by selecting the main points and reporting the main features, and make comparisons where relevant. Write at least 150 words.

A More people are deciding to study professional subjects, such as business, because it gives them a better chance of finding a job.

B The information in the bar chart shows how many undergraduate students chose various subjects at Torrington University in the years 1990 and 2010, and also how many students there were in total for both of these years.

C Torrington University is a good place to study sciences and professional degrees, because these are the subjects which have a growing number of students.

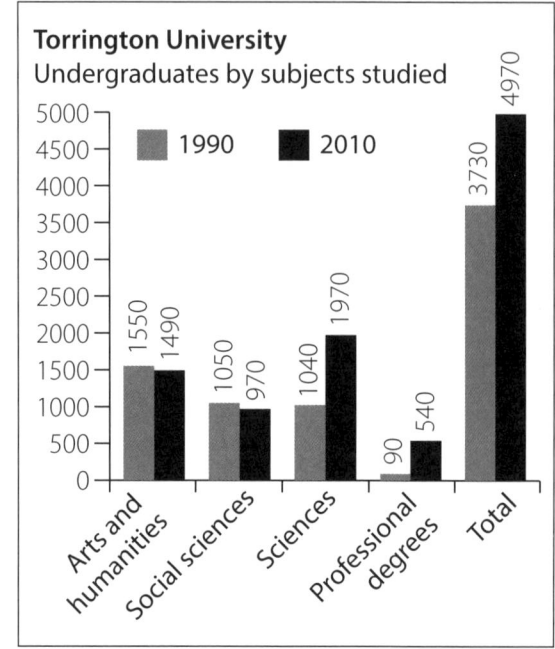

Torrington University
Undergraduates by subjects studied

3a **Work in pairs. Discuss the information you can see in the chart. How was the situation in 2010 different to the situation in 1990?**

3b **Complete the sentences with the information from the chart.**

a) The total number of undergraduates went up to nearly _5,000_ .

b) The number of undergraduates studying arts subjects went down from _____ to 1,490.

c) The number of social sciences students went down from 1,050 to _____ .

d) In _____ , social sciences and sciences had almost exactly the same number of students.

e) The number of students studying sciences went up from _____ to 1,970.

f) The number of students studying professional degrees went up from _____ to 540.

g) No subject had more than _____ students in 1990 or 2010.

4 Look at the model answer. Match the topics (a–d) with the paragraphs (1–4).

a) a paragraph describing what decreased ....2....

c) a final summary of the information ....

b) an overview of the information ....

d) a paragraph describing what increased ....

1 *The information in the bar chart shows how many undergraduate students chose various subjects at Torrington University in the years 1990 and 2010, and also, how many students there were in total for both of these years.*

2 *The number of undergraduate students studying some subjects* **fell** *between 1990 and 2010. The number of undergraduates studying art and humanities subjects* **went down** *from 1,550 to 1,490 and the number of social sciences students also* **decreased***, from 1,050 to 970.*

3 *However, the number of students studying sciences nearly* **doubled** *from 1,040 to 1,970 and the number of students studying professional degrees* **rose** *by more than six times, from 90 to 540. As a result, the total number of undergraduates* **increased** *by about a third to nearly 5,000.*

4 *In conclusion, while the number of arts and social sciences undergraduates* **fell***, the number of postgraduates and undergraduates studying other subjects* **rose** *significantly.*

> **Exam tip**
>
> When you write a description, do it clearly and logically. Make sure that your sentences are written in paragraphs, and that each paragraph has a clear topic.

5 Complete the table with the words in bold from the description.

went up	went down
doubled	

6 Complete the description for this Task 1 question.

EXAM TASK: Writing (Task 1)

The graph shows the percentage of 12-year-old children learning foreign languages in schools in a region of Britain in 1975 and 2015.

Summarise the information by selecting the main points and reporting the main features, and make comparisons where relevant.

Write at least 150 words.

> **Exam tip**
>
> When describing how numbers change, try not to repeat the same words too often. You will get a higher grade if you use a range of vocabulary. Use other words with the same meaning. For example, instead of *went up*, you could say *increased* or *rose*.

Languages learned at school by children, aged 12

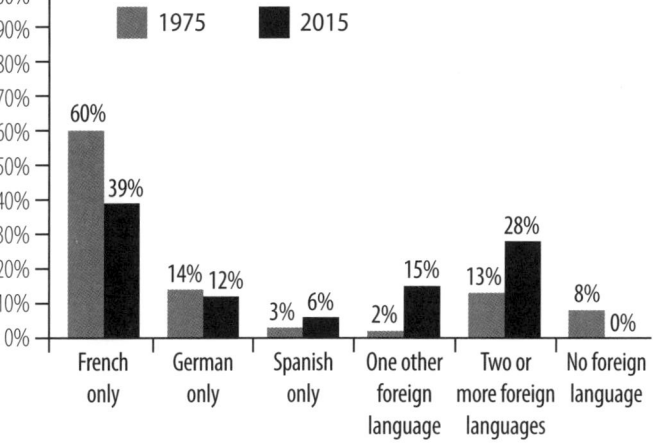

Legend: 1975, 2015

- French only: 60%, 39%
- German only: 14%, 12%
- Spanish only: 3%, 6%
- One other foreign language: 2%, 15%
- Two or more foreign languages: 13%, 28%
- No foreign language: 8%, 0%

The graph gives us information about how many 12-year-old children learned foreign languages in a part of the UK in two years: 1975 and 2015. It also shows the number of children who learned no foreign language.

....

....

....

....

....

....

In conclusion, while the number of children learning French or German decreased, the number of children learning at least one other language, or learning two or more languages increased.

Education issues

1 Work in pairs. Discuss the statements. What are your opinions?

a Some students are stressed at university or school because they study too much.

b Exams are not the best way to test a student's abilities.

c People should only study subjects at university that will lead to a good job.

2 Look at the Task 2 questions below. What are they asking you to do? Match the questions (1–3) with the types of essay (a–c).

1 Some people say that the only reason to study a subject at college or university is in order to get a job related to that subject. Other people say that it more important for students to study subjects they enjoy. Discuss both these views and give your own opinion. ......*c*......

2 Some people say that exams are not the best way to test a student's abilities. Do you agree or disagree? ....

3 Some school children become stressed by their studies. What do you think are the causes of this, and what could be done to solve it? ....

a) Discuss a problem and give some solutions.

b) Discuss the advantages and disadvantages of something.

c) Discuss two opposite points of view and say what you think.

3a Look at the essay plan below, answering question 2 in exercise 2. Match the topics (a–d) with the paragraphs (1–4).

a) Give reasons why you agree with the statement.   ......*2*......

b) Say what you are going to write about.   ....

c) Give your opinion about whether the statement is true.   ....

d) Give reasons why you disagree with the statement.   ....

Paragraph 1: introduce topic / 'In this essay I will discuss ...'

Paragraph 2: exams better for students who are good at exams / stressful, some students don't do well / exams at school don't test skills like dealing with people & being creative

Paragraph 3: we need some kind of system for testing students / imagine doctors, dentists and pilots without exams!

Paragraph 4: exams not always accurate but necessary / not perfect but no other system

3b How are the notes different to normal English?

3c Work in pairs. Read the answer below and discuss the questions.

　　a) Are the ideas in the answer the same as the notes in exercise 3a?

　　b) How many ideas are the same as yours, when you discussed the question in exercise 1?

　　c) Do you agree with the conclusion?

Some people are not sure if exams are really the best way to test a student's abilities. Other people think that there are too many exams, and this is stressful for many students. In this essay, I will discuss this issue and give my own opinion.

Exams are not necessarily the best way to test someone's intelligence. Maybe they only test how good a student is at doing exams. A student who is relaxed in exams may get a much better grade than another student who is very stressed, or just having a bad day. Also, many exams only test a student's knowledge of a subject, or what they have learned in lessons. They do not always test important skills, like dealing with people or thinking creatively.

Of course, it is necessary to have to some kind of system for testing students. Otherwise, there would be no guarantee that a student actually knew anything about a subject. Imagine a world in which doctors, dentists and pilots could do their jobs without being tested in some way.

In conclusion, exams are not a perfect system, but they are the only system we have. They may not always be a totally reliable way to test students' abilities, but they at least give a general idea of what students know. I agree that exams are not always the best way to test students' abilities, but I believe that they are necessary, and I can think of no alternative system which would work better.

Exam tip

Decide what you will write in your last paragraph, before you start writing. This will be your conclusion. If you know what your conclusion is before you start writing, it will help you organise your ideas logically.

4 Work in pairs to write a plan for the Task 2 essay. Decide what your conclusion will be. Then write your essay.

EXAM TASK: Writing (Task 2)

Some people say it is best for children to start learning a foreign language as soon as they start school. Other people say it is better to start later. Discuss both these views and give your own opinion.

You should write at least 250 words.

Property prices

1a **Match the words in the box with the pictures (a–d).**

~~detached house~~   flats / apartments   semi-detached houses   terraced houses

detached house

1b **Work in pairs. Discuss the questions about you and your country. Make sure you understand the words in bold.**

a) What type of **housing** is there in your town?

b) Where are the most expensive places to live?

c) Do most young people **rent** housing or live with their family?

d) Are **property** prices going up or down at the moment?

e) How easy is it to find a place to live in the capital city?

f) Is it easy to take out a **mortgage** to buy a house?

Exam tip

A Task 1 answer needs a short introduction. It should give a general overview of the data. Although the data is usually in the past, the introductory overview is usually written in the present simple tense: *The graph **shows** ... .* Why is it not written in the simple past?

2 **Look at the graph and choose the best introduction for a Task 1 answer. Why is it the best? Discuss your ideas.**

The graph below gives information about property prices in a capital city from 1995 to 2015.

Summarise the information by selecting the main points and reporting the main features, and make comparisons where relevant.

Write at least 150 words.

Average property prices in the capital (1995–2015)

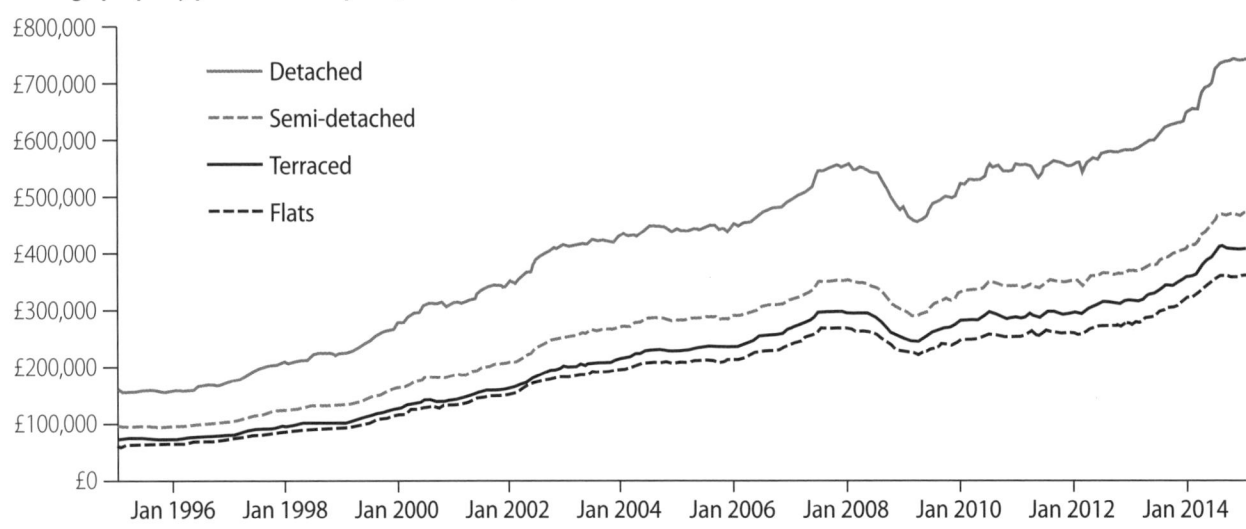

a) The graph gives some very interesting information about a city from 1995 to 2015.

b) The graph shows average property prices in a capital city. There are four lines on the graphs, one for each kind of property, and also some dates. In general, prices increased.

c) The graph shows property prices for a capital city, and how they changed from 1995 to 2015. It gives information for four different types of housing.

3a **Complete these phrases from a Task 1 introduction with a verb beginning with the given letters.**

a) The graph sh.*ows*................... the number of people who …

b) The graph gi................................information about the price of …

c) The graph ill............................. how many people …

d) The graph prov........................... data on the number of …

Exam tip

When you write an introduction, don't use the same words that are in the Task question. Try to give the same meaning with different words, if possible. If you repeat words from the question, it may stop you getting a higher score.

3b **What does *it* mean in the sentence below?**

The graph shows the number of people who bought a house between January and June 2015. **It** also provides information about the age of these people.

4 **Write an introduction for the Task 1 question.**

EXAM TASK: Writing (Task 1)

The graph below shows how much of their income people between 20 and 35 spent on rent, food and bills between 1975 and 2015.

Summarise the information by selecting the main points and reporting the main features, and make comparisons where relevant.

Write at least 150 words.

Percentage of income people aged 20–35 spent on rent, food and bills (1975–2015)

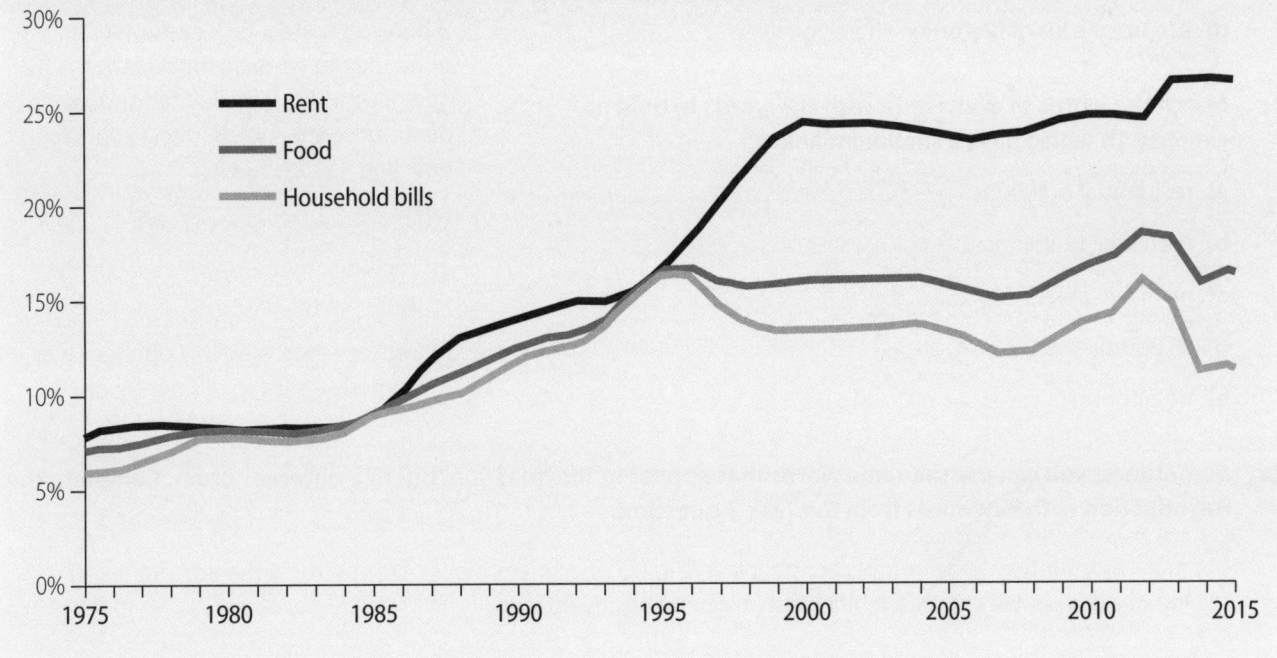

The best place to live

1a **Match the words (1–5) with the photos.**

1) residential buildings ___a___

2) industrial buildings _____

3) an urban area _____

4) a suburb _____

5) neighbours _____

1b **Work in pairs and discuss the questions.**

a) What kind of **accommodation** do you live in?

b) What are the advantages of living in a) **a town or city with lots of people**, or b) **just outside a city centre**?

c) Do you know **the people you live next to**?

d) Are there a lot of **factories** where you live?

1c **Match the words in exercise 1a with the words in bold in exercise 1b which have a similar meaning.**

a) residential buildings: _accommodation_ _____

b) industrial buildings: _____

c) an urban area: _____

d) a suburb: _____

e) neighbours: _____

Exam tip

When you write a Task 2 essay, it's a good idea to write an introduction paragraph. This introduction should paraphrase the question and explain how you will answer it.

What does *paraphrase* mean?

a) repeat something with exactly the same words

b) repeat something in a different way, sometimes using different words

---

2a **Sometimes, you can use the same words that appear in the question, but in a different order. Complete the introduction with key words from the Task 2 question.**

In many <u>city centres</u>, large numbers of people live in <u>tall apartment blocks</u>. Do you think the <u>advantages</u> of living in a city centre apartment block outweigh the <u>disadvantages</u>?

Many people live in **(1)** _tall_ _____ _apartment_ _____ _blocks_ _____ *in* **(2)** _____

_____ *around the world. In this essay, I will discuss whether the* **(3)** _____ *of this*

outweigh the **(4)** _____ .

2b **Look at the underlined key words in this Task 2 question. Complete the introduction with words in the box which have a similar meaning to the key words.**

> In some <u>cities</u>, old <u>industrial buildings</u> have been <u>converted</u> into <u>residential buildings</u>. Do you think this is a <u>positive</u> or a <u>negative</u> development?

> advantages   change   disadvantages   factories and warehouses   ~~houses and flats~~   urban areas

> *Nowadays, there are many* **(1)** _houses and flats_ *in* **(2)** .... *which used to be* **(3)** ....
> *In this essay, I will discuss the* **(4)** .... *and* **(5)** .... *of this* **(6)** ....

3a **Work in pairs or small groups. Choose one of the Task 2 questions below and write an introduction.**

EXAM TASK Writing (Task 2)

a) Some people say that the best place to build new houses is in the countryside, where there is plenty of space. Others say that it is better to build new houses in old industrial areas of cities. Discuss both of these views and give your own opinion.

b) In some cities, housing has become so expensive that key workers such as nurses and teachers cannot afford to live near their places of work. What do you think are the causes of this problem and what could be done to solve it?

c) In some countries, many young working people live in shared houses with similar people. Do you think the advantages of living in a shared house outweigh the disadvantages?

3b **Read the introduction that another pair or group wrote. Discuss the questions.**

a) Does the introduction paraphrase all the key words in the question?

b) Does it avoid using the same words that appear in the question?

c) Does it explain how the writer will answer the question?

4 **Write the rest of your essay for the Task 2 question in exercise 3a.**

- Remember to plan your paragraphs before you write. Make notes in the table below.
- You should write at least 250 words.

Paragraph 2	
Paragraph 3	
Paragraph 4 (Conclusion)	

Sporting activities

1a **Work in pairs. Discuss the questions.**

    a) What are the most popular sports in your country?

    b) How many medals has your country won in each Olympic Games over the last few decades?

    c) Have the numbers of men and women doing sport in your country gone up or down?

    d) Can you explain how doing exercise helps your body?

1b **Imagine you know the answers to the questions in exercise 1a. What would be the best diagrams for showing the information? Match the information to the diagrams below.**

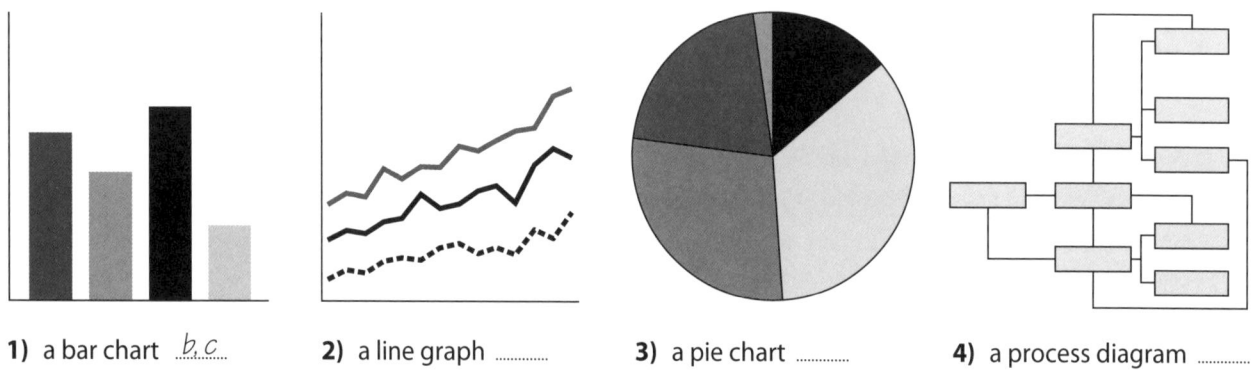

    1) a bar chart _b, c_   **2)** a line graph ....   **3)** a pie chart ....   **4)** a process diagram ....

2 **Look at the chart and the overview sentence below. Which word in the overview means the same as these words?**

The pie chart shows the percentage of children aged 11–16 who do different sporting activities each week in 2012.

    ● proportion ....

    ● share   ....

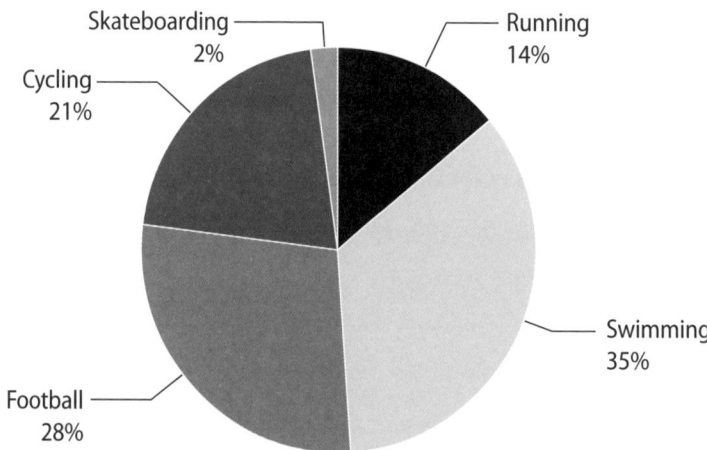

Sports activities done each week by children aged 11–16 in 2012

Skateboarding 2% — Running 14% — Cycling 21% — Swimming 35% — Football 28%

Exam tip

Pie charts usually show percentages. You will get higher score if you use a variety of different words and phrases to describe these percentages. Try to describe the information in the chart using these phrases.

14 percent of children …

The share of children who like swimming is …

The proportion of children who enjoy football is …

The percentage of children who go skateboarding is …

3a Work in pairs. Discuss the two pie charts. What are the biggest changes? What are the smallest changes? What stayed almost the same? Discuss your ideas.

> The two pie charts below show the changes in annual spending by an Australian city on sports facilities and hosting sports events in 2004 and 2014.
>
> Summarise the information by selecting and reporting the main features, and make comparisons where relevant.

Exam tip

Pie charts may have a separate key showing what each area in the chart represents. Make sure you understand what information the pie charts show.

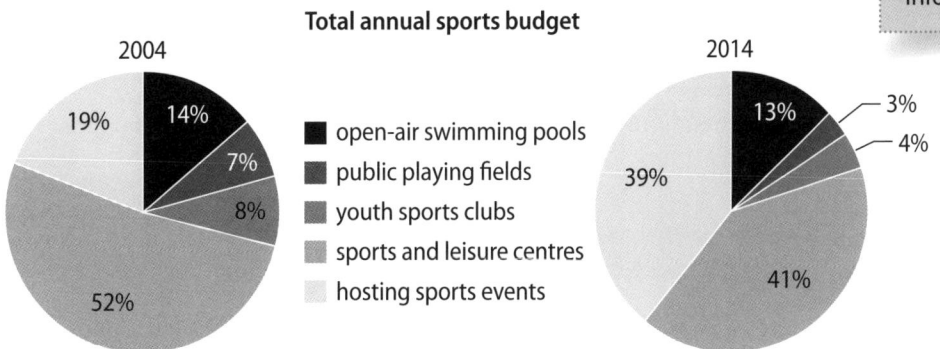

Total annual sports budget

2004 — 19%, 14%, 7%, 8%, 52%
2014 — 13%, 3%, 4%, 39%, 41%

Key:
- open-air swimming pools
- public playing fields
- youth sports clubs
- sports and leisure centres
- hosting sports events

3b Complete the answer with information from the charts.

The two pie charts show the total amount of money spent by an Australian city on sports facilities and hosting sports events in 2004 and 2014.

*The smallest change was the proportion of the budget spent on **(1)** open-air swimming pools. In 2004 the figure was 14%, and in 2014 it had decreased by just **(2)** .... The share of spending on public playing fields decreased from **(3)** .... to **(4)** .... There was also a decrease in the amount of money spent on **(5)** .... The share of the budget dropped from 8% to 4%.*

*The fourth and final decrease was the percentage of the budget spent on sports and leisure centres. In 2004 the figure was 52%, but in 2014 it fell to **(6)** .... Meanwhile, the percentage of the budget spent on hosting sports events increased dramatically. It more than doubled from **(7)** .... in **(8)** .... to **(9)** .... in **(10)** .... This was the largest change in spending.*

4 Write an answer for the Task 1 question.

EXAM TASK Writing (Task 1)

The charts below shows the sporting activities chosen by students at an American high school in 2003 and 2013.

Summarise the information by selecting and reporting the main features, and make comparisons where relevant.

Write at least 150 words.

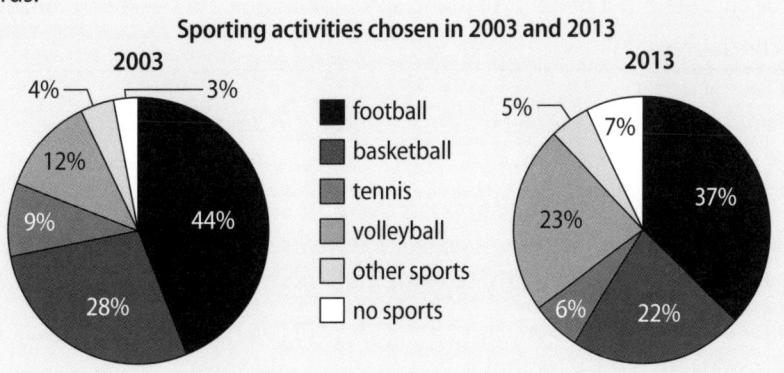

Sporting activities chosen in 2003 and 2013

2003 — 4%, 3%, 12%, 9%, 44%, 28%
2013 — 5%, 7%, 23%, 6%, 37%, 22%

Key:
- football
- basketball
- tennis
- volleyball
- other sports
- no sports

Why do we do sport?

1a   **Work in pairs and discuss the questions.**

a)   What sports can you see in the photos?

b)   Which sports are popular in your country? Are there any other sports which are more popular?

c)   Which sport is the best way to get fit?

1b   **Discuss this Task 2 essay question. What is your opinion?**

Some people say that the only reason to do start doing a sport is to improve health and fitness. Others say that this is not the only reason to start doing a sport. Discuss both these views and give your own opinion.

2   **Work in pairs. Are the statements about Writing Task 2 true or false?**

a)   A Task 2 essay should always start with an introduction. (T)/ F

b)   You don't need to write in paragraphs.   T / F

c)   The essay doesn't need to contain any arguments.   T / F

d)   The essay should end with a conclusion.   T / F

> **Exam tip**
>
> A typical IELTS Task 2 essay ends with a conclusion. Which of the following should never be included?
>
> a)   Your opinion on the topic
>
> b)   A comment addressed to the examiner
>
> c)   A summary of the essay's argument
>
> d)   An additional new point which did not fit with the previous paragraphs.

3a   **Choose the best conclusion for the question in exercise 1b. Why is it the best conclusion? Discuss your ideas.**

Essay plan

Paragraph 1:	introduction, summarise the question
Paragraph 2:	discuss the benefits of doing sports (health and fitness)
Paragraph 3:	discuss the other benefits of doing sport (meeting people, having fun, etc.)
Paragraph 4:	conclusion …?

a)   *In conclusion, I would like to give another reason for starting to do a sport. Sport is very international, and it helps to improve international relations. It can even help to promote world peace.*

b)   *In conclusion, while improving health and fitness is the most obvious benefit from doing sport, it can have many other benefits as well. In my opinion, the health benefits are probably the main reason why most people start doing a sport. The other benefits can also come from many other types of activity.*

c)   *To conclude, I am not interested in sport. Sport is healthy, but I do not need to do sports. I walk three kilometres to work every day, and that is good for me.*

3b **Match the problems with the other conclusions.**

    1) This is too personal, and it does not sum up the main points of the essay. ....

    2) This is a new point. There should not be any new points in the conclusion. ....

4 **Put these parts of a conclusion in the best order.**

    Justify your opinion. ....

    Say which argument you agree with most. ....

    Summarise the arguments from the essay. ....*1*....

5a **Read these conclusions. What do you think the Task 2 question was for each one?**

    a) *In conclusion, computer gaming has some of the characteristics of a sport, **although** in other ways, it is very different. In my opinion, it cannot be considered a sport **because** the majority of computer gaming involves very little physical activity.*

    b) *To conclude, team sports for school children have obvious health benefits, **but** these sports can be dangerous, **as** accidents might happen. **However**, I believe that the health benefits of team sports outweigh any disadvantages for the majority of children. These health benefits may have a positive effect for the rest of their lives.*

5b **Look at the words in bold in exercise 5a. What do they mean? Complete the table.**

but	....
	....
	....
because	....

6a **Work in pairs or small groups. Discuss the Task 2 question below. Which side of the argument do you agree with? Why do you disagree with the other argument?**

EXAM TASK Writing (Task 2)

Some people say that major sports events such as the Olympic Games are good for improving international relations. Others say that these events are too expensive, and we should spend money on other things. Discuss both views and give your own opinion.

Give reasons for your answer and include any relevant examples from your own knowledge or experience.

Write at least 250 words.

6b **Write your conclusion, giving your own opinion.**

Exam tip

Try to write your conclusion in about 40–70 words.

Work and money

1a   Work in pairs. Which jobs are the most useful for society? Which are the least useful? Discuss your ideas.

accountant   shop assistant   tour guide   builder   factory worker   farmer

1b   Match the jobs in exercise 1a with the types of industry.

a) manufacturing *factory worker*   **d)** tourism   ....

b) retail   ....   **e)** financial services ....

c) construction   ....   **f)** agriculture   ....

2a   Look at the Task 1 question and the table and choose the best way to complete the overview sentence.

> The table below shows the number of workers in different industries in four European countries.
>
> Summarise the information by selecting and reporting the main features, and make comparisons where relevant.

Total number of workers by industry (millions)					
	Manufacturing	**Retail**	**Construction**	**Tourism**	**Financial services**	**Agriculture**
Germany	3.57	2.49	2.46	1.97	1.88	0.26
France	2.54	2.52	1.98	3.42	1.59	0.53
Spain	2.58	3.14	2.06	3.01	2.22	0.24
Italy	1.82	1.99	1.5	2.98	0.95	0.47

The table provides information about how many people work in different types of industry, in four countries. In each of the four countries, the total number of workers is …

a) *the same*   **b)** *fairly similar*   **c)** *very different.*

2b   Complete the description with words from the box. In some cases, more than one is possible. Discuss your ideas.

> about   approximately   around   just   nearly   ~~over~~   under

*Germany **has the most** manufacturing workers **at** just **(1)** __over__ .... 3.5 million. France and Spain*

both have (2) .... *2.5 million and Italy has **the fewest at (3)** .... over 1.8 million.*

*In the retail industry, Spain has the most workers, at **(4)** .... 3.15 million. France and Germany*

both have (5) .... *2.5 million, while Italy has just **(6)** .... 2 million. Germany has*

(7) .... *under 2.5 million workers in the construction industry. Spain and France both have **(8)***

.... *2 million, and Italy has **the fewest at** 1.5 million.*

2c Write similar sentences for the other three industries in the table. Use the phrases in bold.

3 Look at the table. What are the main features? Match the jobs to the four categories (a–d) according to the amount of money that men and women earn.

Average annual salaries (thousands of euros)		
Occupation	Men	Women
company director	127.2	98.5
doctor	78.4	75.2
lawyer	69	59.6
accountant	47.3	44
journalist	32.7	29.9
teacher	25	25
secretary	17	26
nurse	19.2	22.7
all jobs	31.3	28.2

Exam tip

In IELTS Writing Task 1, you need to 'summarise the information by selecting and reporting the main features'. If you report every detail in the information, you may lose marks and you may not have enough time to write your Task 2 essay.

Why do we use the phrases in exercise 2b?

a) to describe exact information

b) to summarise the information, sometimes talking about two countries at the same time

a) a big difference _company director_

c) no difference

b) a small difference

d) women earn more

4a Work in pairs. Write an answer for the Task 2 question.

EXAM TASK Writing (Task 1)

The table above shows average annual pay in euros for men and women in eight different jobs.

Summarise the information by selecting and reporting the main features, and make comparisons where relevant.

Write at least 150 words.

Exam tip

The words *approximately*, *around* and *nearly* mean the same as *about*. Use a variety of different words to show the examiner that you have a large vocabulary.

- Write an introduction, saying what the table shows (remember to paraphrase the words in the question).

- Then, write about the jobs where men earn more than women.

- After that, write about the jobs where men and women have the same salary and the jobs where women earn more than men.

- Finally, write a short conclusion (one or two sentences). Give information about the average salaries for all jobs.

4b Compare your description with another pair's. How is it similar? How is it different?

Exam tip

Think about the point the data is making. What is the purpose of presenting this information? This may help you to summarise and select the main points. Remember: you don't need to give your opinion in a Task 1 description.

A fair day's work

1a **Work in pairs or small groups. Look at the photos. Discuss the questions.**

a) What jobs can you see in the photos?

b) In your country, which jobs are usually done by men?

c) Which jobs are usually done by women?

d) Do you think that women can do any jobs that men can do?

e) In your country, are men usually paid more than women?

1b **Read the Task 2 question and a student's introduction. What is the problem with the introduction?**

> Governments should make sure that companies pay men and women the same amount of money for doing the same job. To what extent do you disagree with this statement?

There are very many different types of job. Some are very difficult and some are very dangerous. Some jobs are boring and some are fun. For some jobs, you can get more money. In this essay I will discuss the different reasons for choosing a job, and why money is important.

1c **Which of the ideas (a–f) should not be in an answer to the question in exercise 1b?**

a) a comparison of salaries for women and men in your country

b) the problem of low salaries for nurses and teachers

c) the reasons why salaries for women and men are not always the same

d) the negative effects of unequal salaries for women and men

e) what governments should and should not do to solve the problem

f) the reasons why some occupations have better salaries than others

Exam tip

In IELTS Writing Task 2, it is important that your essay answers the question, and stays on the same topic. Which of these sentences are true about Task 2 essays?

a) You must answer the question fully.

b) You must not cover areas which are not covered by the question.

c) The more ideas you include, the higher the mark you will get.

d) The order you present your ideas is not important.

2a Work in pairs or small groups. Read the Task 2 question. Make a list of the ideas you need to include in your answer.

> In some countries, people work very long hours, and do not have enough free time for leisure and family life. What do you think are the causes of this problem, and what can be done to solve it?
>
> Give reasons for your answer and include any relevant examples from your own knowledge or experience.
>
> Write at least 250 words.

Exam tip

Try to think of relevant ideas for the essay question before you start planning your essay.

2b Listen to other students' ideas. Make notes about any ideas you like and could include in your essay.

2c Work in pairs. Make a plan for the essay. How will you organise your ideas into paragraphs?

2d Compare your plan with the example essay below. Are your ideas the same? What is the focus of each paragraph?

> **1** *In my country, working very long hours has become a common problem, and it seems to be getting worse. Working too much can damage people's health, their relationships and their quality of life. This problem is sometimes referred to as 'work–life balance'. In this essay, I will discuss the cause of this problem, and possible solutions.*
>
> **2** *I think there are two main causes of people working very long hours. The first cause is that employers expect too much. Instead of thinking of their employees as human beings, they think of them as machines, and they want them to do as much work as possible. The second cause is other employees in the organisation. If a person works the minimum number of hours each week, their colleagues may judge that person negatively for not doing their fair share of work.*
>
> **3** *I think the solution is very simple. Every job should have a contract with a fixed number of hours. People could work extra hours if they wanted to, but they would receive extra pay for this. I believe that this would be better for employees and better for the employers. In my opinion, relaxed, happy people usually do better work than tired, stressed people.*
>
> **4** *In conclusion, I think that problems with work–life balance are caused by the expectations of both employers and employees. The best way to solve this problem would be to have contracts with fixed hours, and to encourage people not to work longer than they need to.*

3a Make a plan for the Task 2 essay.

EXAM TASK: Writing (Task 2)

For some people, being happy is the most important reason for choosing a job. Other people think that having a good salary is more important. Discuss both these views and give your own opinion.

Give reasons for your answer and include any relevant examples from your own knowledge or experience.

Write at least 250 words.

3b Use your plan to write the essay.

Exam tip

The IELTS test in general is based on a range of 'typical' topic areas. Some of the most popular are work, education, the environment, tourism, heath, cities, leisure activities and the media. Knowing these typical topic areas can help you to build your vocabulary of useful words for writing about those topics.

Problems and their causes

1 **Work in pairs. What are the environmental problems? What causes them?**

a) air pollution　　　　**b)** flooding　　　　**c)** melting ice caps

2a **Work in pairs. Look at the Task 1 question and the diagram. Match the words (1–8) with the definitions (a–h).**

> The diagram shows the main reason why global warming causes the oceans to rise.
>
> Summarise the information by selecting and reporting the main features, and make comparisons where relevant.
>
> Write at least 150 words.

1 glacier	**a)** to turn to liquid
2 iceberg	**b)** a very large piece of ice on land
3 to melt	**c)** to help something move (oil is a common way to do this)
4 to lubricate	**d)** a large piece of ice in the sea
5 to flow	**e)** the top of something
6 surface	**f)** to increase
7 to rise	**g)** how high the sea is
8 sea level	**h)** to move

The effect of rising air and sea temperatures on glaciers

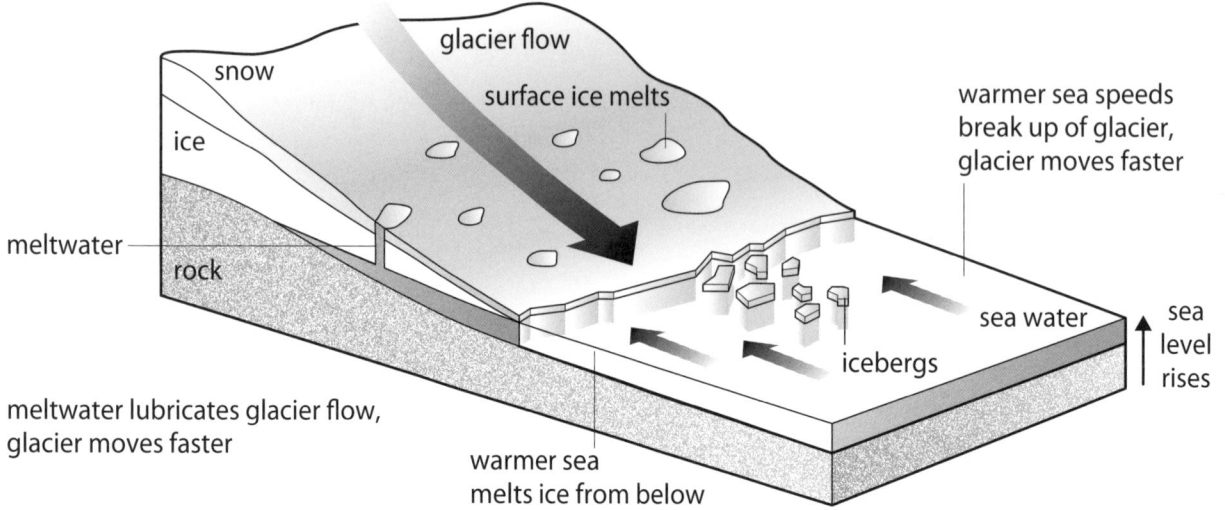

glacier flow

snow

surface ice melts

ice

warmer sea speeds break up of glacier, glacier moves faster

meltwater

rock

sea water

icebergs

sea level rises

meltwater lubricates glacier flow, glacier moves faster

warmer sea melts ice from below

2b Look at the diagram again. There are two processes. Number the sentences in the best order to describe the processes.

Process 1		Process 2	
The glacier breaks up into icebergs.	....	The sea level rises.	....
The glacier flows into the sea faster.	....	The top of the glacier melts.	....
The sea level rises.	....	The meltwater lubricates the flow of the glacier.	....
The glacier flows into the sea.	*1*	The glacier flows into the sea faster.	....
The sea melts the glacier.	....	The meltwater goes down through the glacier.	....

2c Look at the words in bold in the sentences. Why do we use them?

This **causes** the glacier to break up into icebergs.

Because of this, meltwater goes down to the rock below.

The result is that the sea level rises.

a) to explain why something happens

b) to give our opinion about something.

2d Complete the description with words from the diagram and *cause*, *because* and *result*.

The diagram shows how rising sea and air **(1)** *temperatures* .... cause glaciers to melt faster. It shows the point where a glacier meets the sea and breaks up into **(2)** ....

The glacier flows from the land into the sea. At the point where the glacier is partly in the sea, the warmer sea temperature means that the glacier melts from below faster. This **(3)** .... it to break up into icebergs more quickly. **(4)** .... of this, the glacier flows into the sea faster.

At the same time, the rising air temperatures cause the **(5)** .... on the surface of the glacier to melt faster. The meltwater from the surface snow travels down through the ice to the rock below. This water **(6)** .... the flow of the glacier over the rock. The **(7)** .... of this is that the glacier moves into the sea faster. All of these things **(8)** .... the sea level to rise.

Exam tip

There may be more than one process in a diagram. When you first look at a diagram, decide:

- How many processes are there?
- What is the main cause of each process?
- What is the final result of each process?

3 Write a description of the Task 1 diagram.

EXAM TASK: Writing Task 1

The diagram shows the process which results in acid rain, and its effects.

Summarise the information by selecting and reporting the main features, and make comparisons where relevant.

Write at least 150 words.

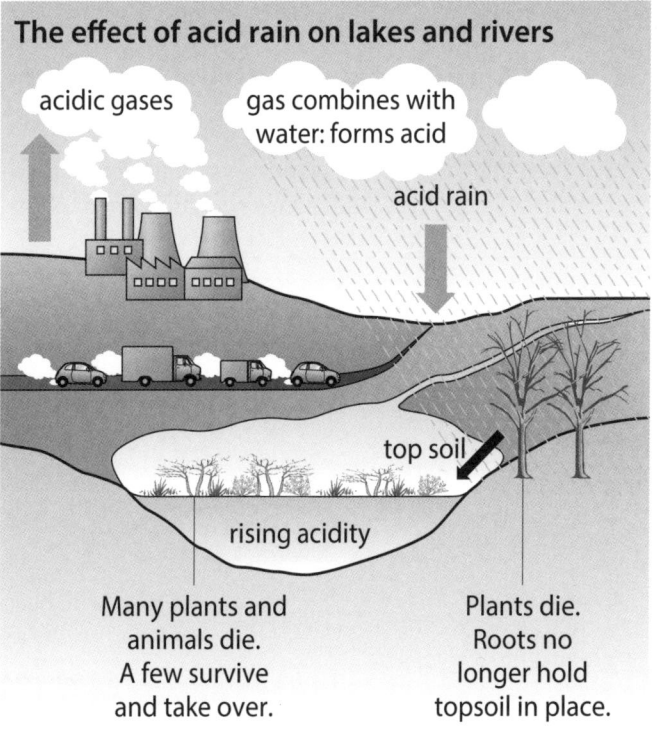

The effect of acid rain on lakes and rivers

acidic gases

gas combines with water: forms acid

acid rain

top soil

rising acidity

Many plants and animals die. A few survive and take over.

Plants die. Roots no longer hold topsoil in place.

Looking after the planet

1a   Work in pairs. Do you agree or disagree with the statements? Why/Why not?

a We should not have zoos, because it is cruel to keep animals in cages.

b Petrol should be more expensive, so people use their cars less.

1b   Work in different pairs. Discuss the statements again. This time, one of you must agree with the statement. The other one must disagree with it.

2   Work in pairs. Read the paragraph from an answer to the Task 2 question. Discuss why it is not a good paragraph.

> Animals should not be kept in zoos, because it is cruel to keep them in cages. To what extent do you agree or disagree?

> *It is cruel to keep animals in small cages, but nowadays most modern zoos keep the animals in large areas, not cages. There are some endangered species which are now only in zoos. The zoos save them from extinction. However, there are still some bad zoos, with small cages. Those are not good. It is sad to see animals in small spaces. People enjoy visiting zoos, and they are educational for children. Bad, old-fashioned zoos should close, but I believe that modern zoos are a good thing.*

Exam tip

In IELTS Writing Task 2, you may have a statement, followed by 'To what extent do you agree or disagree?'

A good way to answer this type of question is to explain why you agree in the second paragraph, then explain why you disagree in the next paragraph.

Why is it important that the arguments in an essay are not mixed up together?

3a   Work in pairs. Discuss the statement. Complete the table with a list of reasons and examples to agree and disagree with the statement.

> Protecting the natural world, and endangered species such as pandas and tigers, is very expensive and not always successful. The money should be spent on helping humans instead.

agree	disagree

PHOTOCOPIABLE

3b Read the paragraph agreeing with the statement. Does it match your reasons and examples?

(1) *It is true that protecting endangered animals is expensive and sometimes a waste of money.* (2) *For example, in parts of Asia there are areas where tigers can live safely, and many people work to stop them being killed. However, a lot of other people kill tigers every year.* (3) *We can spend lots of money on protecting animals, but some people think that spending money to protect them is only delaying the time when they become extinct. For that reason, some people think it is better to spend money on things like schools and hospitals instead.*

3c Find the parts of the paragraph which do these things.

a) give examples ......2...... **b)** justify the argument .... **c)** introduce the argument ....

4a Now write a similar paragraph which disagrees with the statement in exercise 2a.

4b Swap paragraphs with another pair. Does their paragraph introduce the argument, give examples and justify the argument? Help them to improve it if necessary.

5 Look at the paragraph from an answer to the Task 2 question below. It has a clear argument, but there is another problem with it. What do you think it is?

Petrol should be more expensive, so people use their cars less. To what extent do you agree or disagree?

I absolutely disagree that the price of petrol should be higher. Nobody would be able to afford to drive to work or to take their children to school. Everybody would have to stay at home. Nobody would have any fun. They would have to spend all their money on petrol just to drive a few kilometres, and they would never have any money to spend on food. Raising the price of petrol would be the worst solution for everybody.

Exam tip

When you write an IELTS essay, avoid giving very strong or exaggerated opinions. In IELTS, it is better to give both sides of an argument first, and give your opinion at the end.

6 Read the Task 2 question. Plan each paragraph. Remember that for each main paragraph you should introduce the argument, give examples and justify the argument. Use the plan to write the essay.

EXAM TASK: Writing (Task 2)

Many people think that animals should not be used by people for food, research or work. To what extent do you agree or disagree?

Give reasons for your answer and include any relevant examples from your own knowledge or experience.

Write at least 250 words.

Paragraph 1: Introduction	
Paragraph 2: Give arguments agreeing with the statement	
Paragraph 3: Give arguments disagreeing with the statement	
Paragraph 4: Conclusion	

The circle of life

1a   **What animals can you see in the pictures?**

1b   **What do you know about these animals' life cycles (how they grow up, from baby to adult)?**

2   **Complete the description of the life cycle of the frog with the words in the box.**

> ~~after~~   eventually   finally   first   point

Frogs lay their eggs in water. **(1)** _After_ a while, the tadpoles come out from the eggs. At **(2)** ...., these tadpoles have no legs, but then the legs start to grow. **(3)** ...., the tadpole looks like a small frog with a tail. At this **(4)** ...., it is called a 'froglet'. **(5)** ...., the tail disappears and the frog has its adult shape. The next stage is that the female frog lays some eggs, and the process begins again.

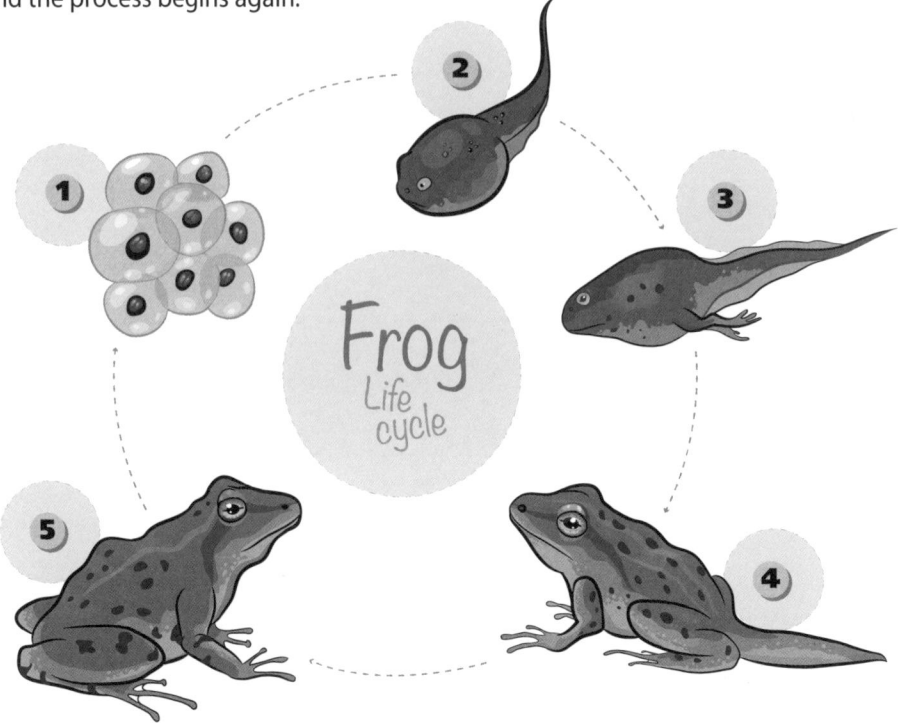

Frog
Life
cycle

3 **Work in pairs. Look at the Task 1 question and answer. Add linking words to the answer.**

The diagram below shows the life cycle of an insect called the cicada.

Summarise the information by selecting and reporting the main features, and make comparisons where relevant.

Write at least 150 words.

The life cycle of a cicada

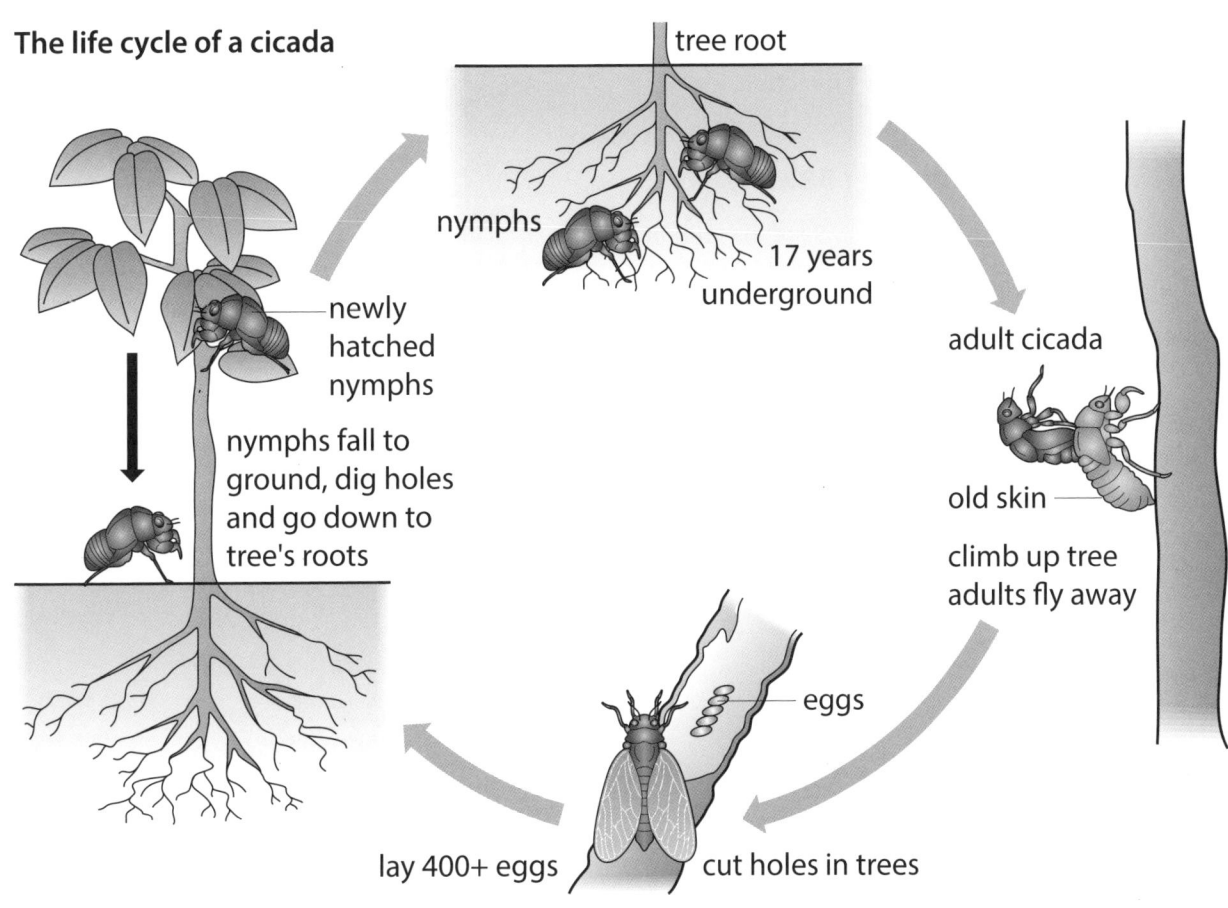

The diagram shows the life cycle of the cicada. It is divided into four main stages.

In the diagram, the cycle begins with nymphs, which are the immature form of the cicada. These nymphs live under the ground in the roots of trees. **(1)** *After* seventeen years, the nymphs come up from below the ground, **(2)** .... they climb up the tree they were living under. **(3)** .... , the adult cicada emerges from the skin of the nymph. **(4)** .... , the cicadas fly away. **(5)** .... , the female cicadas return to a tree. **(6)** .... each one lays more than 400 eggs in holes which they have cut into the surface of the tree. The nymphs fall to the ground **(7)** .... they hatch out of the eggs. Finally, the nymphs dig holes in the ground and go down under the tree, **(8)** .... go into the tree's roots. They live there for another seventeen years, **(9)** .... the cycle begins again.

Exam tip

Make sure you understand the diagram correctly. Don't start writing until you are sure you have understood all the parts.

---

4   **Work in pairs or small groups and follow the instructions.**

   a)   Look at the diagram below. Do you already know anything about this topic? What is the most logical point to start a description of the cycle?

   b)   Plan a short presentation to describe the process. Use linking words.

   c)   Work with another pair and take turns to give your presentation. Were the presentations clear and easy to understand? Did they use linking words?

5   **Write an answer for the Task 1 question.**

EXAM TASK: Writing (Task 1)

The diagram below shows the life cycle of the salmon.

Summarise the information by selecting and reporting the main features, and make comparisons where relevant.

Write at least 150 words.

Exam tip

An IELTS Writing Task 1 diagram may have some vocabulary which you don't know. It is usually possible to work out the meaning from the context. For example, in this diagram, it's not necessary to know exactly what *reeds* and *gravel* are. It's enough to know that they are things at the bottom of a river.

Life cycle of a salmon

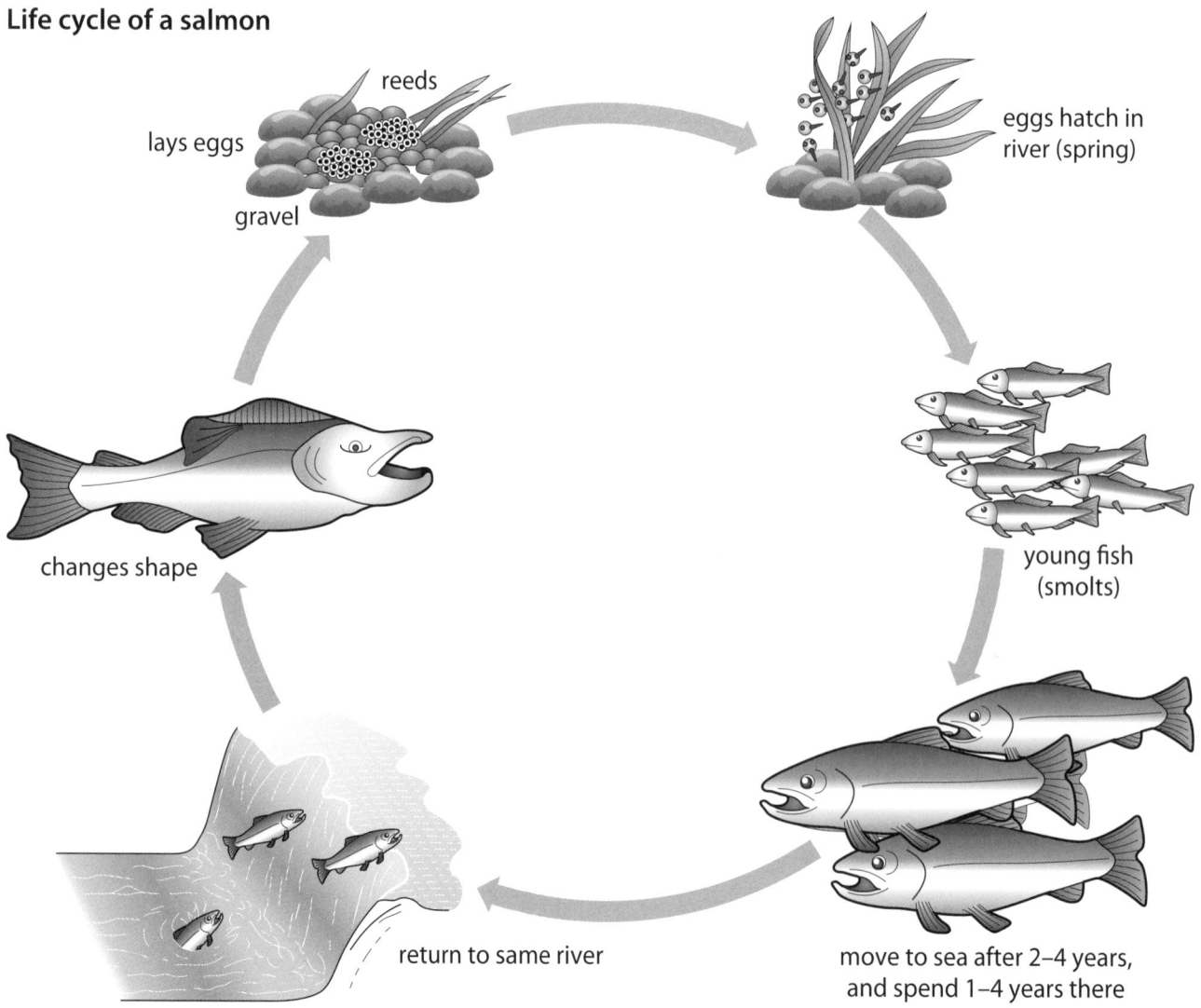

lays eggs — reeds — gravel

eggs hatch in river (spring)

young fish (smolts)

move to sea after 2–4 years, and spend 1–4 years there

return to same river

changes shape

Solving the problem

1 **Work in pairs. Look at the photos and discuss the questions.**

a) Do many people suffer from these problems in your country?

b) Discuss possible solutions for each of the problems.

2a **Which sentences are talking about solutions to problems? Which are talking about causes of problems?**

a) Many illnesses and health problems **are due to** lack of sleep.

b) Stress **causes** many health problems.

c) Banning sugary drinks would **result in** better health for millions of people.

d) Doing more exercise often **leads to** better health.

2b **Complete the essay with the phrases in the box.**

> a simple solution to this problem   as a result   ~~due to~~   is a result of
> the most common reason for   this would mean that

> Many people do not get enough sleep, and this can affect both their health and their happiness. What do you think are the causes of this problem, and what measures could be taken to solve it?

*Many people feel tired for much of the time **(1)** due to* .... *lack of sleep, and this can be bad for their health and their happiness. In this essay, I will discuss the reasons for this problem and give a solution.*

*Many people have busy lives. They have to work, buy and cook food, look after children and look after old relatives and do many other things. At the same time, they also want to enjoy leisure activities such as sport, being with friends and doing hobbies. All these things can take up a lot of time, and there may not be enough hours in the day. **(2)** ...., their days get longer and their nights get shorter. I believe that this is **(3)** ....* lack of sleep.

*In my opinion, there is **(4)** .... People should try to be less busy in their daily lives.* **(5)** *..............................they have more time for sleep. To be less busy, people need to change how much they do in one day. For example, if someone invites them out in the evening, they should say no, because it is more important to get a good night's sleep.*

*In conclusion, lack of sleep **(6)** .... trying to do too much in one day. I believe that deciding to do fewer things in a day could help people to solve this common problem.*

Exam tip

In IELTS Writing Task 2, you may be asked to write a problem–solution essay. This is often about a common social problem, and ends with 'What do you think is the cause of this problem, and what could be done to solve it?' or words with a similar meaning.

What other common social problems can you think of? Share your ideas.

Exam tip

There are lots of fixed phrases which are useful for IELTS Writing Task 2 essays. Write them in your notebook. A good way to do this is to write example sentences, and underline the useful phrase. For example:

Many people do not switch their phones off at night. As a result, they do not get enough sleep.

3a   Work in pairs. Look at the Task 2 question. Complete the table with causes for children around the world becoming overweight and possible solutions.

EXAM TASK: Writing (Task 2)

More and more children around the world are becoming overweight. This can affect their health and happiness. What do you think are the causes of this problem, and what could be done to solve it?

Give reasons for your answer and include any relevant examples from your own knowledge or experience.

Write at least 250 words.

causes	solutions

3b   Discuss your ideas from exercise 3a, using the phrases below.

Causes

● A major cause of .... is/are ....

● Another reason for this problem is ....

● .... is also a reason for this problem.

Solutions

● A simple solution is ....

● Another possible solution is ....

● .... could also help to solve the problem.

4   Write an essay for the Task 2 question in exercise 3a. Remember to write an introduction paragraph first, and a conclusion paragraph at the end.

Exam tip

Time yourself when you practise writing an essay. You will have 40 minutes in the exam. Allow 5 minutes for planning, 25–30 minutes for writing and 5–10 minutes to check your writing at the end.

PHOTOCOPIABLE

How was it made?

1. **Work in pairs. Discuss the questions.**

   a) What can you see in the photos?

   b) What are the things made of? (e.g. glass, concrete, paper, etc.)

2. **Complete the sentences using the passive form of the verbs in bold.**

   a) People **made** the cups from glass.

   The cups *are made* .... from glass.

   b) Someone **melts** the glass and then **turns** it into special shapes.

   The glass .... and then it .... into special shapes.

   c) Someone **folds** the paper and **changes** its shape.

   The paper .... and its shape ....

   d) People **built** the tower in the 1950s.

   The tower .... in the 1950s.

   e) People **used** concrete to make the tower.

   Concrete blocks .... to make the tower.

Exam tip

In IELTS Writing Task 1, you may be asked to describe how something is made. We often describe processes using the passive voice. We do this when we are more interested in the thing that was made, rather than who made it.

How do you think the things in the photos were made?

Exam tip

The passive can very useful for describing manufacturing and production processes, but if you only use the passive, you may lose marks for not using a variety of grammar.

3a **Look at the diagram. Match the words (1–6) with the definitions (a–f).**

1 limestone

2 furnace

3 molten

4 mould

5 recycled

6 cooling

a) a machine for making thing very hot

b) a shape in which something is made

c) a type of rock

d) melted

e) becoming colder

f) used again

> The diagram shows the process for manufacturing glass bottles.
>
> Summarise the information by selecting and reporting the main features, and make comparisons where relevant.
>
> Write at least 150 words.

How bottles are made

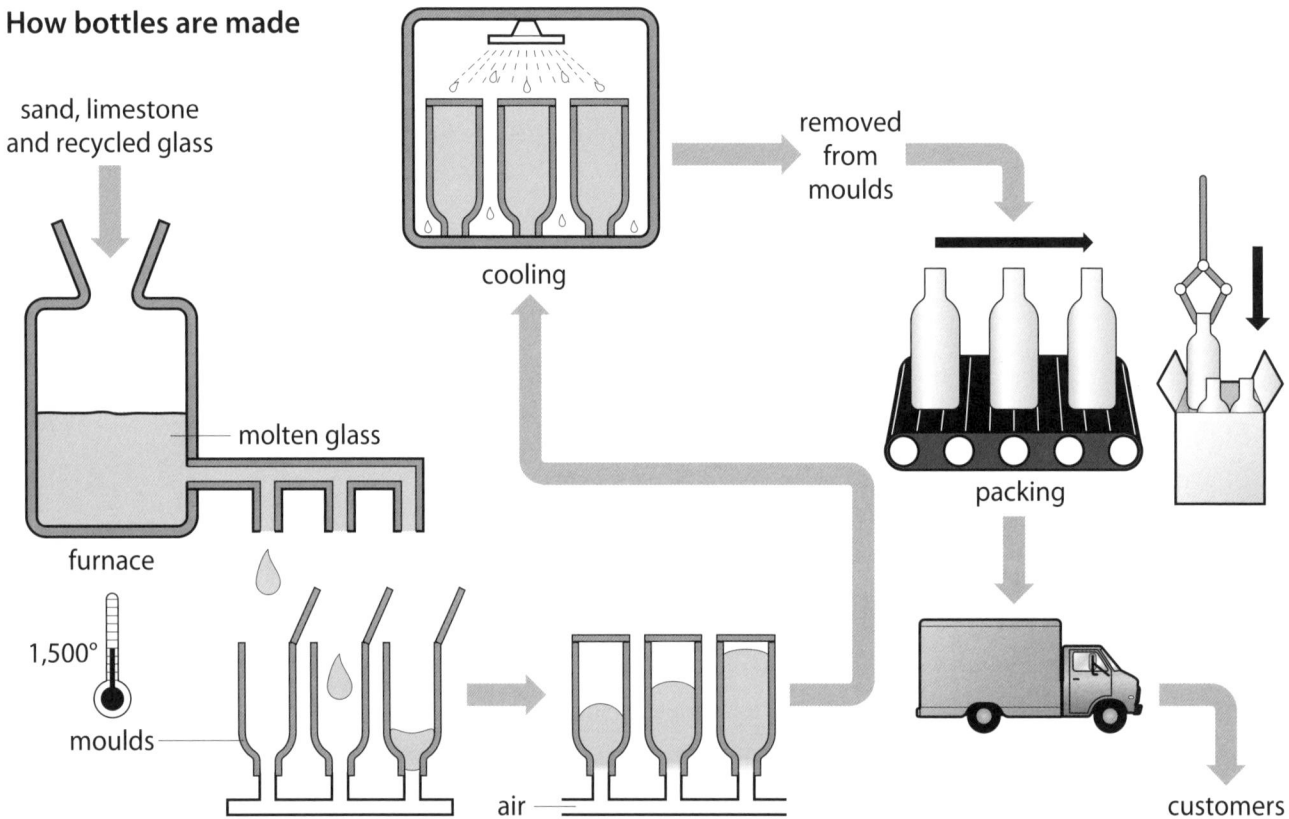

3b **Complete the model answer with the passive form of the verbs in brackets.**

The diagram shows the process for making glass bottles. It is divided into four main stages.

First of all, sand, limestone and recycled glass **(1)** *are put* .... *(put) into a furnace together and then they*

(2) .... *(heat) to 1,500 °C. This creates molten glass. Then, small amounts of this molten glass*

(3) .... *(put) into moulds. These moulds have the shape of bottles. These moulds*

(4) .... *(fill) with air, and this air makes the molten glass bigger, until it completely fills the moulds.*
Now the molten glass is in the shape of bottles.

Next, the moulds **(5)** .... *(cool) with water, so the glass becomes solid. After this, the bottles*

(6) .... *(remove) from the moulds and then they* **(7)** .... *(send) to the packing*
area. They arrive in the packing area. Then, they **(8)** .... *(put) into boxes by a machine.*

Finally, the bottles **(9)** .... *(load) onto a lorry and* **(10)** .... *(take) to the customer.*

4 Look at the diagram in exercise 5. Match the words (1–5) with the definitions (a–e).

1 cement

2 quarry

3 kiln

4 to grind (past form: ground)

5 to crush

a) a machine for making things very hot

b) to make into a powder

c) a place where rock is taken from the ground

d) to break into small pieces

e) something used to make concrete, using in building

5 Write an answer for the Task 1 question.

EXAM TASK: Writing (Task 1)

The diagram below shows the process for manufacturing cement.

Summarise the information by selecting and reporting the main features, and make comparisons where relevant.

Write at least 150 words.

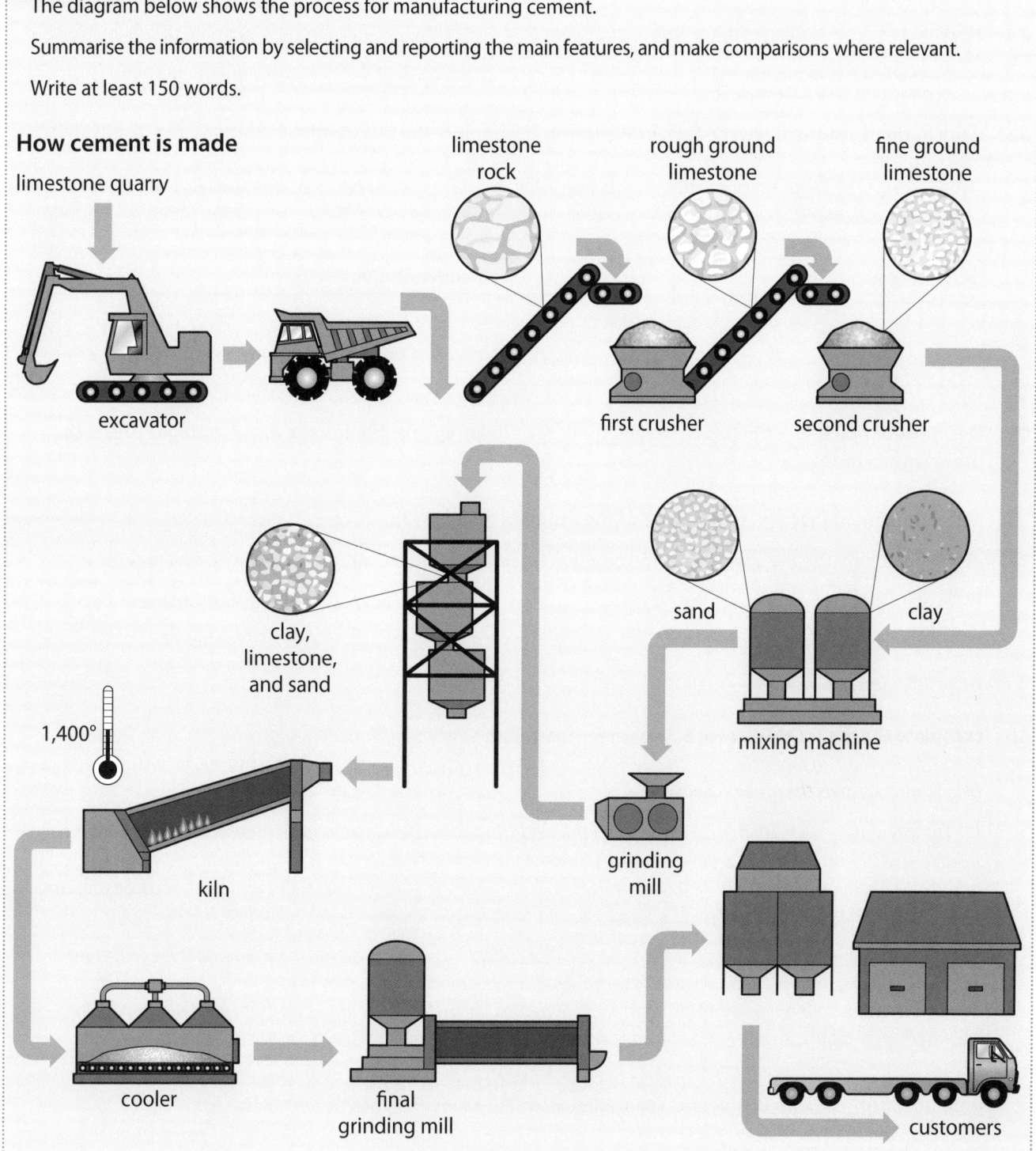

How cement is made

limestone quarry

excavator

limestone rock

rough ground limestone

fine ground limestone

first crusher

second crusher

clay, limestone, and sand

sand

clay

mixing machine

1,400°

kiln

grinding mill

cooler

final grinding mill

customers

Online shopping

smartphones

online shopping

Exam tip

In IELTS Writing Task 2, you may be asked to write an essay discussing the advantages and disadvantages of something. It often includes the phrase 'to what extent do the advantages outweigh the disadvantages?'.

What do you think *outweigh* means here?

1   **Work in pairs and discuss the questions.**

a) What are the advantages of the things in the photos?

b) What are the disadvantages?

2a   **Work in small groups. Read the Task 2 question and complete the table with advantages and disadvantages.**

> Nowadays some children spend many hours every day using smartphones and other devices. The disadvantages of allowing children to own these devices outweigh the advantages. To what extent do you agree or disagree?

advantages	disadvantages

2b   **Decide your opinion on the topic. Do you think the advantages outweigh the disadvantages or is it the other way round?**

2c   **Match the functions (a–g) to the parts of the example essay (1–7).**

a) briefly summarise the advantages and disadvantages ......*5*......

b) explain how you will answer the question   ....

c) introduce the question topic   ....

d) justify your final opinion   ....

e) describe the disadvantages   ....

f) describe the advantages   ....

g) give your final opinion   ....

> **(1)** *Smartphones and other devices have become a part of daily life for millions of people, and this includes children. Some children spend many hours each day using these devices.* **(2)** *In this essay, I will discuss the advantages and disadvantages and give my own opinion.*
>
> **(3)** *The internet can help children to learn about the world and it can be educational in other ways too. Children will need to know how to use digital devices and the internet later in their lives, and it is useful to start learning at an early age. Also, children who do not have digital devices and access to the internet may suffer at school, because they are different to their classmates.*
>
> **(4)** *Although using digital devices has many benefits for children, spending too much time doing this can be bad for them. It is very important for children to do other activities such as sports, playing with their friends and reading books. If they miss out on these other important experiences and activities, it may stop them from developing into healthy, happy adults. Another disadvantage is that they may visit websites which are not suitable for children.*
>
> **(5)** *In conclusion, it is necessary for children to have digital devices so they can learn about and be part of the modern world, but there are some dangers too.* **(6)** *In my opinion, the advantages of children having digital devices outweigh the disadvantages, but parents should check how much time their children spend using digital devices, and how they use them.* **(7)** *Otherwise it may cause serious problems for their development.*

Exam tip

Before you start planning an advantages/disadvantages essay, make a list of advantages and disadvantages.

If you have too many advantages and disadvantages, it may make your essay too long to write in the time available. Choose the most important points. Two or three advantages and two or three disadvantages are usually enough.

3a Work in pairs. Read the Task 2 question and complete the table with advantages and disadvantages of online shopping.

EXAM TASK: Writing (Task 2)

In many countries, online shopping has become very popular and is still increasing in popularity. The advantages of shopping online far outweigh the disadvantages. To what extent do you agree or disagree with this statement?

You should use your own ideas, knowledge and experience and support your arguments with examples and relevant evidence.

You should write at least 250 words.

advantages	disadvantages

3b Decide your opinion on the topic. Do you think the advantages outweigh the disadvantages or is it the other way round?

3c Write a Task 2 essay answering the question in exercise 3a in about 40 minutes.

- Write the introduction to the essay. Paraphrase the question title and explain how you will answer it.

- Write a paragraph describing the advantages.

- Write another paragraph describing the disadvantages

- Write your conclusion. Briefly summarise the advantages and the disadvantages. Give your final opinion and justify it.

This place has really changed!

1 **Work in small groups. Ask your partners about their home town or city.**

a) How has it changed recently?

b) What new buildings have been built?

c) Have any old buildings been knocked down or repaired?

d) Has the transport system changed? How?

2a **Work in pairs. Look at the maps and discuss the questions.**

a) What are the maps?

b) What features can you see in the maps?

c) What information do the maps give us?

d) What are the main differences between the two maps?

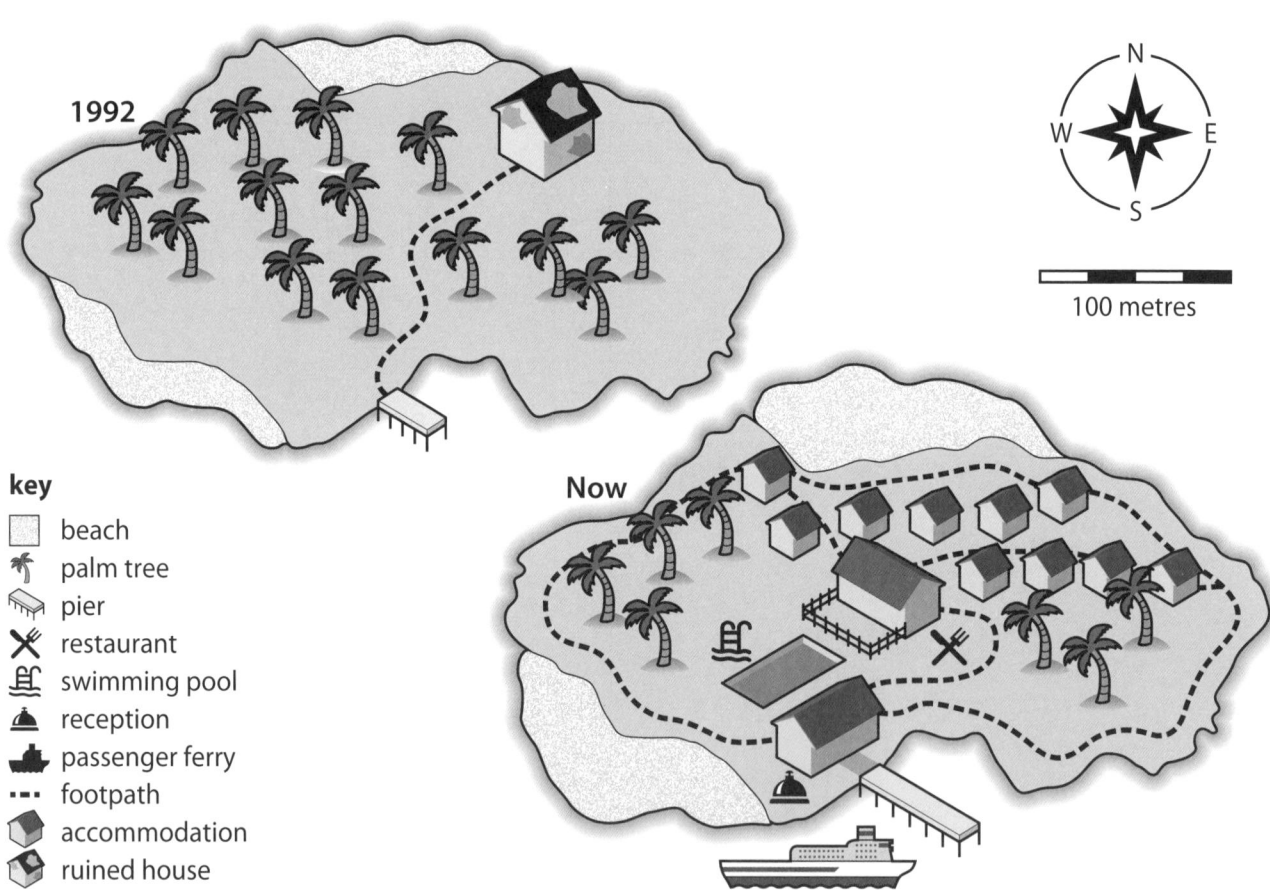

1992

Now

100 metres

key

- beach
- palm tree
- pier
- restaurant
- swimming pool
- reception
- passenger ferry
- --- footpath
- accommodation
- ruined house

2b **Are the statements about the maps true or false?**

a) The beaches are the same size in both maps. T / **F**

b) The pier was longer in 1992. T / F

c) There were more trees in 1992. T / F

d) There are more buildings now than in 1992. T / F

e) One building from 1992 is no longer on the island. T / F

f) The new buildings are all accommodation. T / F

3a Look at the *Now* map again. Complete the sentences with the present perfect or present simple forms of the verbs in brackets.

a) The ruined house *has gone* .... (go).

b) Now a path .... (go) around the outside of the island.

c) Some of the trees .... (disappear).

d) Both beaches .... (grown).

e) Now the pier .... (be) longer.

3b The present perfect passive can be useful for describing changes which have a result in the present. Complete the sentences with the present perfect passive form of the verbs in brackets.

a) The ruined house *has been demolished* .... (demolish).

b) Some of the trees .... (cut down).

c) A big restaurant .... (build).

> **Exam tip**
>
> In Task 1 questions with maps, make sure you mention all the important features. There may also be some drawings which are there to help you understand the maps better. In the example in exercise 2a, notice the ferry coming towards the island.

4 Work in pairs. Look at part of a Task 1 question and example answer below. In the answer find:

a) three mistakes in the information

b) three mistakes in the grammar

c) one piece of information which is not relevant, because it does not describe the changes.

> The two maps show the seafront area of a town before and after it was redeveloped.

The two maps show how the seafront area of a town changed when it was redeveloped. It compares the area as it is now with exactly the same area three years ago.

The pier was been demolished, and the beach is now much wider than it was. Three years ago there is a road behind the beach, but now this has gone. It has been replaced with a cycle track. There is a small picture of a bicycle on the cycle track and a small picture of a person on the footpath. Three years ago, the rest of the area in the map was a car park. In the middle of the car park, next to the road, there was a hotel. Now the park has been changed into a car park, and the hotel has been changed to a visitor centre. North of the visitor centre, an art gallery has built. In the middle of the park, there is now a boating lake.

Before it was redeveloped, the area was mainly for cars. Now it is for pedestrians and cyclists.

Three years ago

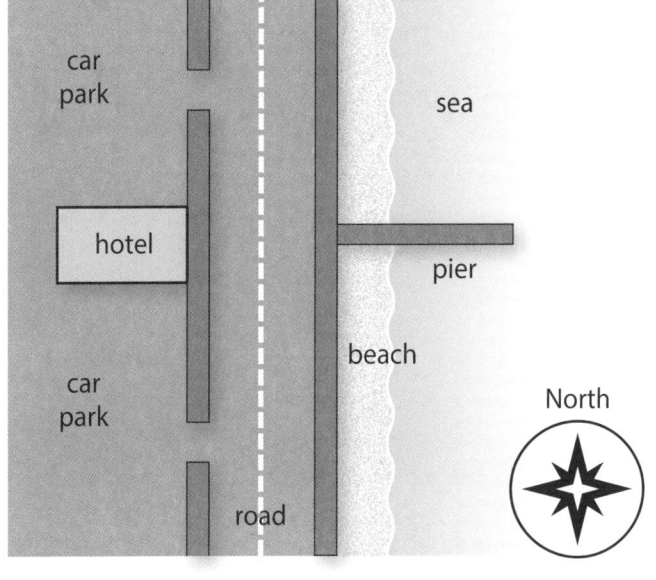

Now

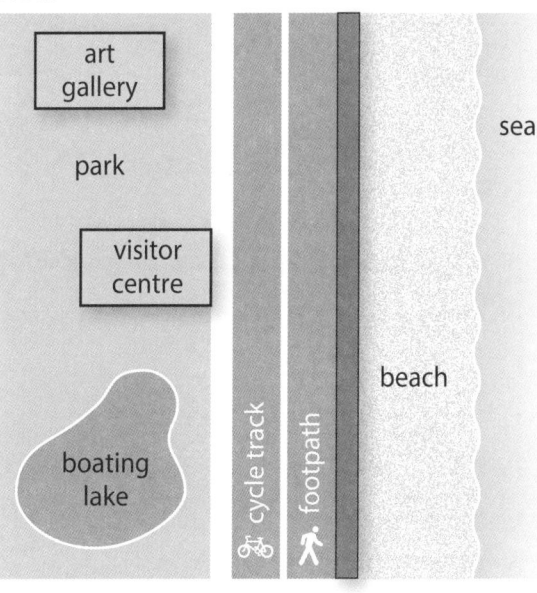

5a   **Read the Task 1 question. Look at the maps and make notes in the table.**

EXAM TASK: Writing (Task 1)

The two maps show a lake before and after it was redeveloped as a facility for tourists

Summarise the information by selecting and reporting the main features, and make comparisons where relevant.

Write at least 150 words.

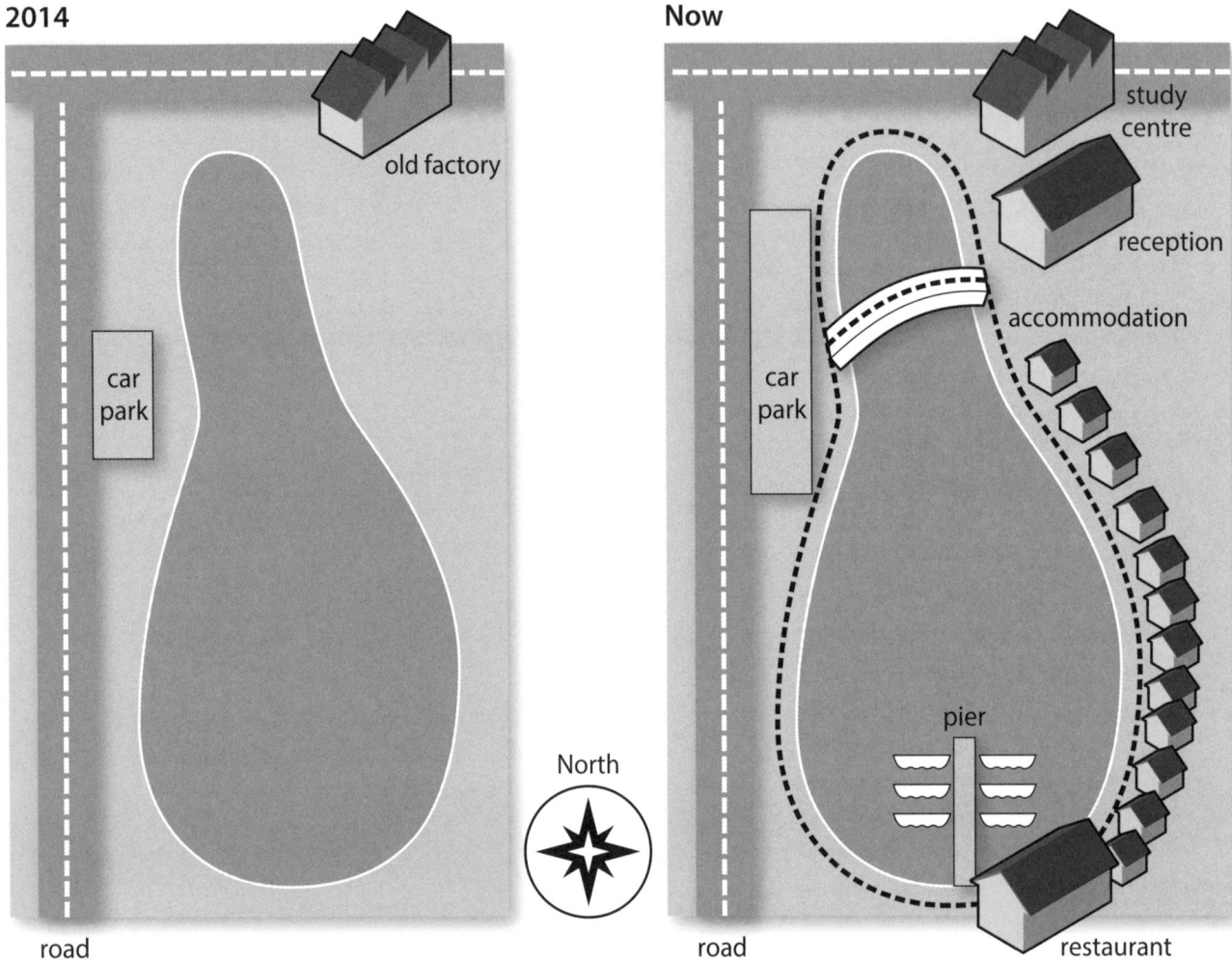

2014	Now

5b   **Use your notes to write the essay.**

The tourist dollar

1a **Work in pairs. Ask and answer the questions.**

a) What types of holiday do people in your country enjoy?

b) What did you do for your last holiday? Why?

c) Where would you like to go for your next holiday?

1b **Discuss the statements. Do you agree or disagree?**

1 It's nice to go away on holiday. It's nice to come home again.

2 Holidays are fun. They can help you to learn more about the world.

3 Tourists spend a lot of money. Tourism is an important part of a country's economy.

Exam tip

You can use linking words to write longer sentences and to connect sentences with each other. You may lose marks if your essay is all in short, unconnected sentences.

What other linking words do you know? Can you make example sentences with them?

2a **The sentences in exercise 1b are simple, but they could be linked together. Connect the ideas with the linking words in the box. Sometimes there is more than one possible answer.**

> although   but   however   while

a) It's nice to go away on holiday, _but / although_ it's nice to come home again.

b) It's nice to go away on holiday. _____ , it's nice to come home again.

c) _____ it's nice to go away on holiday, it's nice to come home again.

> also   and   in addition

d) Holidays are fun _____ they can help you to learn more about the world.

e) Holidays are fun. They can _____ help you to learn more about the world.

f) Holidays are fun. _____ , they can help you to learn more about the world.

> because   so   therefore

g) Tourists spend a lot of money, _____ tourism is an important part of a country's economy.

h) Tourists spend a lot of money. _____ , tourism is an important part of a country's economy.

i) _____ tourists spend a lot of money, tourism is an important part of a country's economy.

j) Tourism is an important part of a country's economy _____ tourists spend a lot of money.

Exam tip

Don't start a sentence with *and*, *but* and *so* in academic writing. You can use *therefore*, *however* and *in addition* to start a sentence, but you can't use these words in the middle of a sentence.

3 **Look at the Task 2 question and follow the instructions.**

a) Work in pairs. Rewrite the essay below so the sentences are longer and better connected with each other.

b) Join another pair and compare your essays. How did you link sentences? What words did you use?

c) Compare your version with the example answer.

EXAM TASK: Writing (Task 2)

Tourism is not always good for the people who live in popular holiday destinations. It can have a negative effect on their lives. To what extent to you agree with this opinion?

Give reasons for your answer and include any relevant examples from your own knowledge or experience.

Write at least 250 words.

Tourism is a very important industry all over the world. A holiday is the best part of the year for many people. Tourism often does not benefit local communities as much as it could.

Tourism creates many jobs. Most of these are not well paid. Many jobs in tourism are only for the summer season. These jobs are better than no job. They often do not bring much money to local people.

Tourists spend a lot of money. People think tourism benefits local businesses. A lot of the money that tourists spend does not benefit local businesses. It goes to big companies who own most of the shops, hotels and restaurants. Some of the money tourists spend may not even benefit the country they are visiting. It goes to international companies. Some tourists try to spend money with small local businesses. Many tourists are not aware of this problem.

Many tourists respect local customs and behave in a responsible way. Some do not. Some tourists do not learn about local customs before they visit a country. They do not know what will upset local people. This may not seem very important. Tourists' behaviour can make local people unhappy.

In conclusion, I agree that tourism does not always benefit local people. The big companies which make money from tourism should pay their workers more. Tourists should try to spend more money with local businesses. Tourists should have more respect for local customs.

The news today

1 **Work in pairs. Discuss the questions. Give reasons for your answers.**

a) Has the number of newspapers and TV stations in your country gone up or gone down recently?

b) Are more or fewer people buying newspapers than 10 years ago?

c) Are more or fewer people watching TV than 10 years ago?

2a **Look at the table and answer the questions.**

a) What does the table show?

b) How has the number of younger readers changed?

c) How has the number of older readers changed?

d) How has the total number of readers changed?

> The table below shows the number of readers by age of a national newspaper in 2000 and 2015. Summarise the information by selecting and reporting the main features, and make comparisons where relevant.

Readers (000s) by age group in 2000 and 2015		
Age	**2000**	**2015**
Under 20	65	5
20–34	110	35
35–49	195	175
50–64	355	370
65+	280	345
Total	**1,005**	**930**

2b **Complete the overview sentence with words from the box.**

> the years   age groups   total number of   ~~how many people read~~   data

The table gives information about **(1)** _how many people read_ a national newspaper. The **(2)** .... shows different **(3)** .... for **(4)** .... 2000 and 2015. It also shows the **(5)** .... readers for those years.

Exam tip

When you write the overview in IELTS Writing Task 1, it is very important that you don't just copy words from the question. Try to use other words and phrases, if possible.

3a **Work in pairs. Look at the rest of the answer. How is it repetitive?**

> The number of readers under 20 **went down** from 65,000 to 5,000. Readers aged 20 to 35 **went down** from 110,000 to 35,000. Readers aged 35 to 49 **went down** from 195,000 to 175,000. Readers aged 50 to 64 **went up** from 355,000 to 370,000. Readers aged 65 and over **went up** from 280,000 to 345,000. The total **went down** from 1,005 to 930. In summary, the table shows that the number of readers aged below 50 **went down** while the number of readers aged 50 and older **went up**.

3b   Take turns to say a sentence from the paragraph in exercise 3a. Replace *went up* and *went down* with words from the table.

went up	went down
increased	decreased
rose	dropped
	fell

> The number of readers under 20 fell …

Exam tip

In IELTS Writing Task 1, you can get a better score by using a wider range of words and phrases to describe numbers and trends.

Do you know any other words which mean *go up* and *go down*?

4a   Look at the words in the box. Which words mean *by a lot*? Which word means *by a little*?

> slightly   dramatically   significantly   considerably

4b   Repeat exercise 3b, but this time add one of the words to each verb.

> The number of readers under 20 fell dramatically …

Exam tip

Phrases with a verb plus an adverb (*fell dramatically, increased slightly*) can also be written as adjective plus noun: *there was a dramatic rise … , there was a slight increase … .*

5   Choose the correct options to complete the answer.

The number of readers under 20 **(1)** significant fall / fell significantly from 65,000 to 5,000. This was the most **(2)** fell dramatically / dramatic fall. Readers in the 20 to 34 age group also **(3)** decreased significantly / significant decrease, falling by a large amount from 110,000 to 35,000. Readers aged between 35 and 49 **(4)** dropped slightly / slight drop from 195,000 to 175,000. In contrast, readers from the ages of 50 to 64 **(5)** increased slightly / slight increase from 355,000 to 370,000 and there was a **(6)** rose considerably / considerable rise in readers over 65.

6   Write an answer for the Task 1 question.

EXAM TASK: Writing (Task 1)

The table below shows the number of visitors to a news website and their average annual income in 2006 and 2016.

Summarise the information by selecting and reporting the main features, and make comparisons where relevant. Write at least 150 words.

Average visitors per week (000s) in 2006 and 2016 by annual income		
Annual income	**2006**	**2016**
Under €15,000	34	67
€15,000–€29,999	45	101
€30,000–€44,999	50	52
€45,000–€59,999	42	15
€60,000+	34	9
Total	**205**	**244**

Old and new media

1 **Work in pairs. Discuss the questions.**

a) How much time do you spending visiting websites each day?

b) What do you think of advertisements on websites?

c) Do you know what an ad-blocker is? Do you use one?

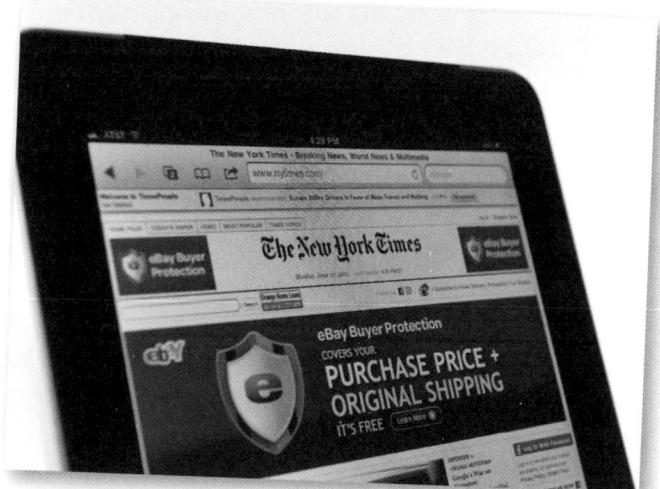

Exam tip

IELTS Writing Task 2 questions often ask you to 'include any relevant examples from your own knowledge or experience'. This means that you can use examples from your own life to support your arguments.

Did you give examples when you discussed the questions above? If you did, what were those examples?

2 **Read the Task 2 question. Are the examples of relevant examples from your own knowledge or experience (1–6) suitable (S) or not suitable (NS)?**

Many websites have advertisements. Some people say this is annoying because there they make websites difficult to use. Other people say that these advertisements are necessary, because they create money for the websites.

Discuss both views and give your own opinion. Give reasons for your answer and include any relevant examples from your own knowledge or experience.

Write at least 250 words.

1) *I have little personal knowledge or experience of this topic, but I believe that ...* $\mathcal{S}$

2) *Just yesterday, I was trying to book a train ticket online, and the website was really slow. I think this was because of the time it took for all the adverts to load. It took about ten minutes just to buy my ticket!* ....

3) *Using an ad-blocker has improved my own personal experience of using the internet.* ....

4) *I am not interested in computers, and I do not know anything about this topic. Instead, I will discuss advertising in general.* ....

5) *Ad-blockers are one of the most popular types of browser extension. They work across all major operating systems, except for some browser versions which are only for smartphones and tablets.* ....

6) *Ad-blocking software is free, easily available and has been downloaded by millions of people.* ....

Exam tip

The examiner will expect your 'relevant examples from your own knowledge or experience' to be written in the same academic style as the rest of the essay. Do not write in a conversational style.

3a Work in pairs. Read the Task 2 question, then discuss the questions below.

EXAM TASK: Writing (Task 2)

Around the world, the sales of newspapers are declining as people increasingly get the news from the internet instead. Is this a positive or a negative development?

a) How do you find out about the news? Which of the ways shown in the photos do you use the most?

b) How often do you buy a real newspaper? Has this changed?

c) What do you like about reading a real newspaper?

d) What do you like about getting news from the internet?

3b Think about why sales of newspapers are going down, and why more people are getting news from the internet. Complete the table with notes based on your own knowledge and experience.

Facts I know about this topic	My personal experience of this topic

3c Work in pairs. Look at the essay outline below. Discuss how you can follow the instructions to write the essay.

Paragraph 1	Introduce the topic and explain how you will answer the question.
Paragraph 2	Explain the benefits of getting news from websites. Explain why many people prefer to get news from the internet rather than buy a newspaper. If your own habits have changed, you can mention this.
Paragraph 3	Explain the benefits of real newspapers. Compare the experience of reading a newspaper with visiting a website. Compare the quality of journalism in newspapers and websites. Make comparisons based on your own knowledge/experience, if you can.
Paragraph 4	Say if you think the decline of newspapers and the increase of internet news is a good thing, a bad thing or neither. Explain why.

Exam tip

Describing your personal knowledge and experience must not be the main purpose of a Task 2 essay. The main purpose must be a more general discussion of the topic. Just use your personal knowledge and experience to support your arguments.

4 Write a Task 2 essay answering the question in exercise 3a. Include examples from your own knowledge and/or experience if possible. Write at least 250 words.

Changing cities

1 Work in small groups. Discuss how your town or city has changed in the last 10 to 20 years. Use the ideas in the photos and your own ideas.

2 Match the graphs (A–F) to the summaries (1–6).

> **Exam tip**
>
> In IELTS Writing Task 1, you may have to describe a line graph. This can be difficult, because you cannot describe every detail of each line. You have to summarise the data.
>
> Look at the charts below, and think of ways to summarise them.

A

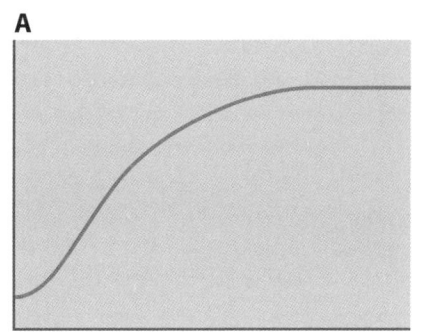

B

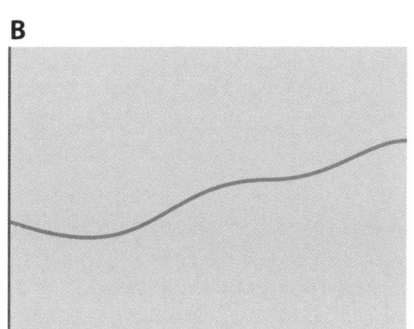

C

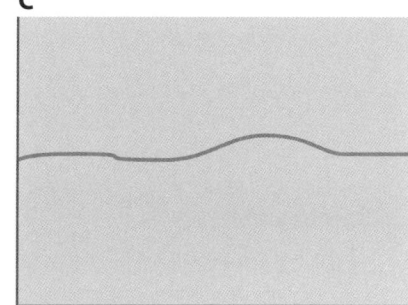

D

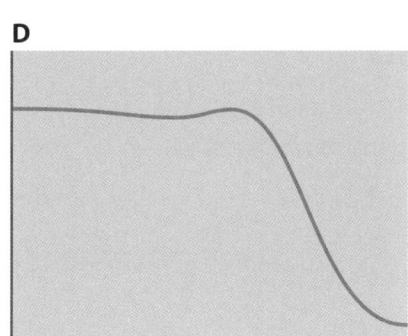

E

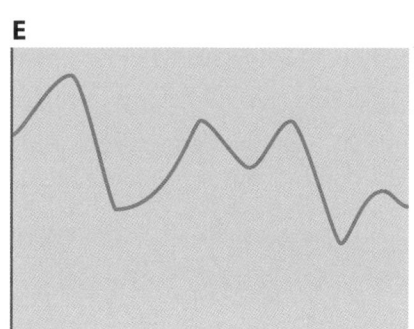

F

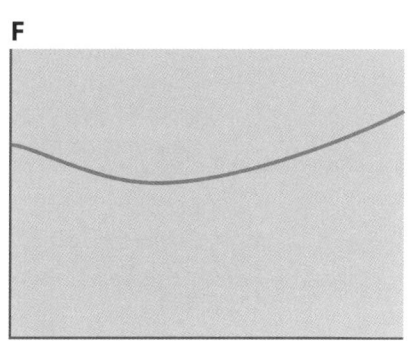

1) in general, the figure rose ....*B*....

2) the figure stayed fairly level ....

3) the figure fell slightly then gradually increased again ....

4) the figure rose, then levelled off ....

5) the figure stayed level, then suddenly fell ....

6) the figure fluctuated, but in general it went down ....

> **Exam tip**
>
> There are many ways to describe lines on a graph. For an IELTS score of up to 5.5 it is enough to know a small number and to use them properly.

3a Read the answer to a Task 1 question. Draw a line on the graph for each city, and write the name of that city near the line.

The chart shows population changes in three European cities over the last century.

The population of Minz was just under 3 million in 1900. It fell to around 2 million in the 1920s, then stayed fairly level until it started to rise again in the 1960s. It continued to increase, and at the end of the century it was about 3 million.

The population of Deaubourg fluctuated until the 1950s, but in general it went down. Then it gradually increased, and from around 1990 it started to rise more quickly. By 2000 it had reached almost 2 million.

In 1900, Arnchurch had a population of less than a quarter of a million. It stayed fairly level until around 1960, then it rose quickly. In 1970 it levelled off at about 2 million, then in the late 1980s it started to rise again. Towards the end of the century, it levelled off at just below 4 million.

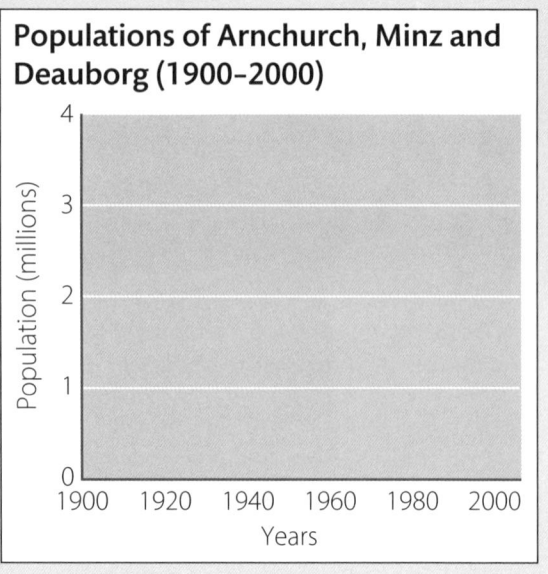

Populations of Arnchurch, Minz and Deauborg (1900–2000)

3b Underline words and phrases for giving approximate figures in the answer.

4 Do the Task 1 question. Use the words and phrases in the boxes to help you.

EXAM TASK: Writing (Task 1)

The chart shows the changes in population in the three European cities between 1900 and 2000.

Summarise the information by selecting the main points and reporting the main features, and make comparisons where relevant. Write at least 150 words.

Barnheim: around 200,000   rose quickly   levelled off at around 2 million
started to rise again in the 1960s   continued to rise

Astbury: increased gradually until about 1950   reached around 1.5 million
started to fluctuate   in general, the population increased

Couville: around 1.3 million in 1900   gradually decreased   started to rise around 1970
reached around 1.5 million   started to decline again

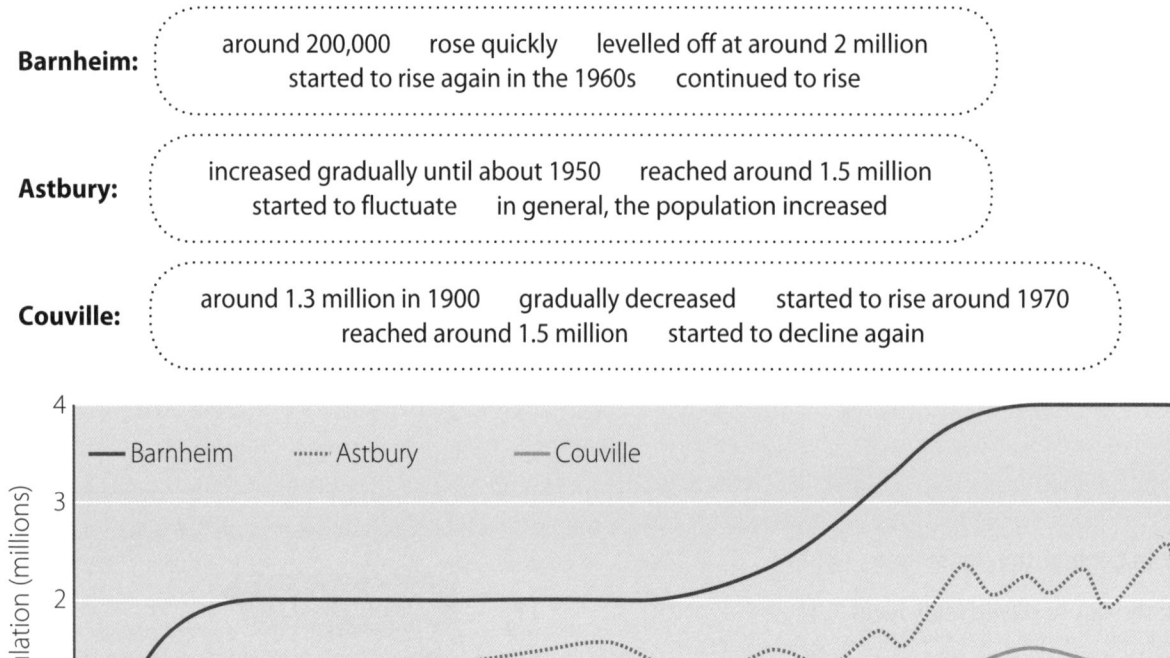

Crowded cities

1 **Work in pairs. Discuss the questions.**

a) Have you ever written an essay for work, school or university?

b) Did you find it easy to write? Why?/Why not?

c) In your language, is there a difference between writing in an academic style and writing to a friend? How would you explain the difference?

2 **Work in pairs. Decide if examples (a–g) are suitable (S) or not suitable (NS) for an IELTS Task 2 essay.**

a) Addressing the reader: *If you have never visited New York, I really recommend it.* _NS_

b) Starting a sentence with a linking word: *However, visiting New York can be expensive.* ....

c) Exaggeration: *New York is the most exciting, most wonderful city in the whole world. No other city is as good.* ....

d) Comparison based on facts: *New York has more popular tourist attractions than perhaps any other city in the USA.* ....

e) Repeating ideas. *New York is a stressful city. It is stressful because so many people live there. New York always feels stressful.* ....

f) Exclamation marks: *It would be impossible to see everything in New York in one visit!* ....

g) Making a statement without supporting it: *New York is a strange city.* ....

3 **Look at the example essay. Underline one example of each of the following mistakes.**

a) addressing the reader

b) exaggeration

c) a repeated idea

d) a statement with no support to justify it

e) an unclear point

> **Exam tip**
>
> An academic English style avoids informal words and aims to give ideas simply and clearly. Use an academic style of English to write your IELTS essays.
>
> Look at these examples. Which is informal and which is neutral?
>
> **a)** You should visit my city. You'll love the amazing museums and fantastic restaurants!
>
> **b)** The number of museums and restaurants in my city has increased significantly in the last few years, perhaps because of the increase in tourists.

Life is incredibly stressful for everybody who lives in a city. In this essay, <u>I will tell you about</u> the causes of this problem and some possible solutions.

In my opinion, there are three main causes of stress for people who live in cities. The main cause is that cities tend to be crowded, and many people find this stressful. Maybe people are travelling a lot, but I don't know where. A third reason for stress is that cities can be very expensive places to live. Not having enough money can feel very stressful for some people.

One solution for the problem of city stress is to move out of the city. However, it is not possible for most people to leave their work and their home. They cannot easily leave their jobs and the places where they live. A more realistic solution would be to make working hours less fixed. This could help to reduce the rush hour crowds, and this could make life less stressful for many people. Another solution would be to increase pay for people who live in cities, so they feel less stressed about money. Cities are so strange.

Much of the stress of city life is caused by too many people and not enough money. Making cites feel less crowded and giving people who live in cities more money might help to solve this problem.

4a Write an answer to the Task 2 question. Write an introduction, two main paragraphs and a conclusion. Base the two main paragraphs on the conversation below. Try not to make any of the mistakes in exercise 3.

EXAM TASK: Writing (Task 2)

Around the world, many cities are growing fast. Just over half of the world's population now lives in an urban area, and this is expected to increase significantly in the future. Is this a positive or a negative development?

Give reasons for your answer and include any relevant examples from your own knowledge or experience.

Write at least 250 words.

> I think the main reason cities are getting bigger is people moving there from the countryside. I think that's a good thing. Cities are where most of the jobs and most of the interesting things to do are. Who really wants to work in the fields all day? It's easy to see why lots of people want to move to a city instead.

> Yeah, that's true, I suppose, but there are loads of problems with big cities too. It's stressful, and there's often a lot of pollution, and there's often awful poverty too, even in cities in rich countries. And some of these cities are getting *much* too big. You get kids who've never seen the countryside. It's not a natural way to live.

4b Swap essays with a partner. Check each other's essays to make sure they are in an academic style.

4c Make any changes you need to your essay.

City transport

1 **Work in groups. Look at the photos and discuss the questions.**

a) What can you see in the photos?

b) What types of transport do you use most often?

c) Do you regularly travel to a place of work or study? If so, how?

d) Which do you think are the best types of transport for travelling in a city? Why?

Exam tip

In IELTS Writing Task 1, you may have to compare figures with each other.

In your group, how many people own a bicycle? How many people own a car? Make a sentence to compare these two statistics.

2a **Work in pairs. Look at the bar chart. Discuss the questions.**

a) What does it show?

b) What was the most popular form of transport?

c) What was the least popular?

Daily commuter journeys by transport type in the city of Renzburg, 2015

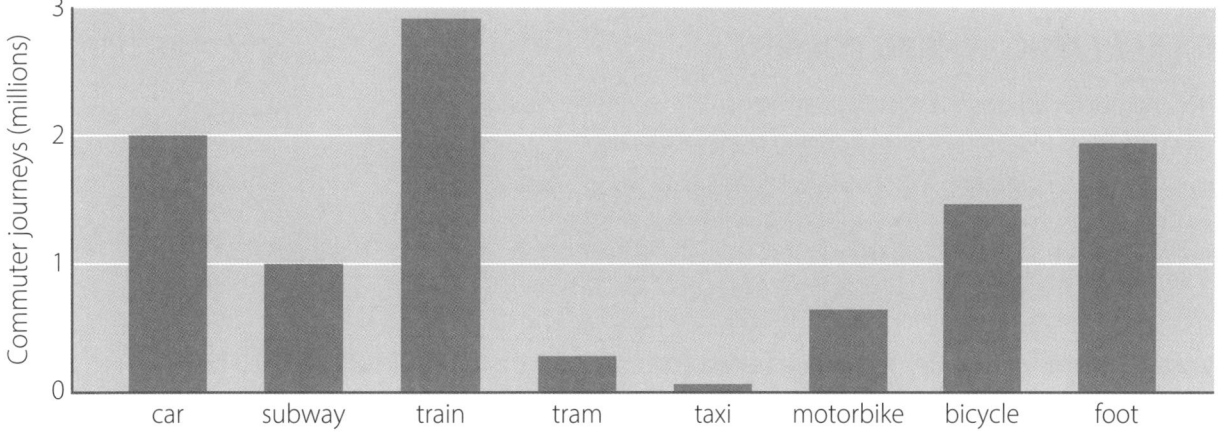

2b **Complete the sentences about the bar chart with the correct forms of transport.**

a) Nearly three million people travelled by _train_........................... , while just over a third as many travelled by ....

b) Around two thirds of a million people went by .... to work, while about double that number went by ....

c) Approximately two million people went by .... to work, just slightly more than the number who went on ....

d) The least popular form of transport was travelling by .... Around three times as many commuters went by .... and ten times as many used the ....

3a Read the description and complete the chart.

Approximately one million commuters drove their cars to work, while **twice as many** went by subway. **Just over** half a million people travelled to work by train, but **around three times that number** went by tram. Only **around** 100,000 people commuted by taxi, while **nearly five times that number** went to work by motorbike. The most popular form of transport was the bicycle, with **just under** three million people cycling to work. **Two thirds as many** people travelled on foot, making that the second most popular way to get to work.

Daily commuter journeys by transport type in the city of Hanbai, 2015

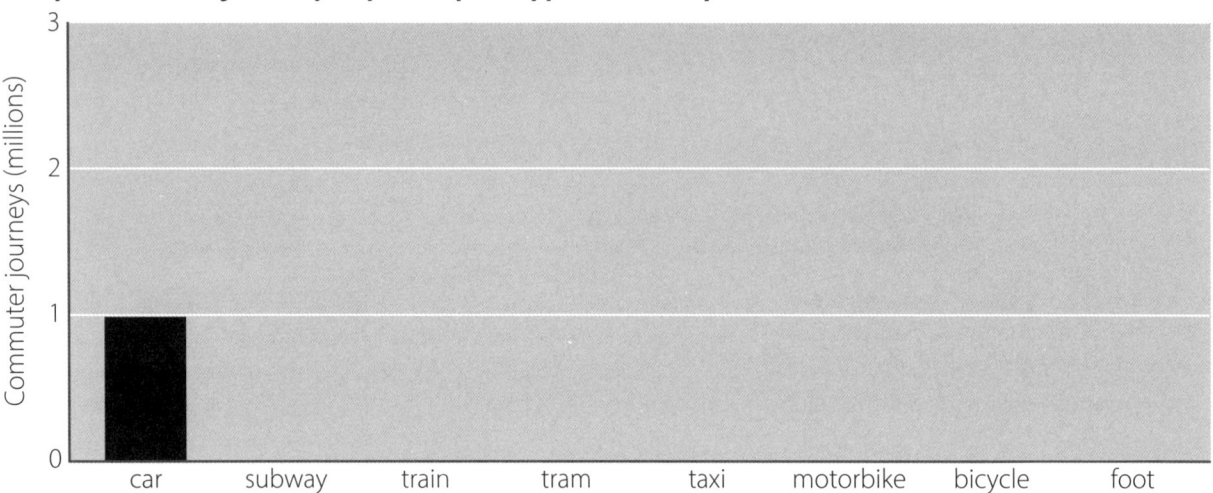

3b Complete the table with the words and phrases in bold from exercise 3a.

Giving approximate figures	Comparing figures
approximately	*twice as many*

4 Write an answer for the Task 1 question.

EXAM TASK: Writing (Task 1)

The chart below shows the average number of journeys taken using different types of transport in a European city in 1985 and 2015.

Summarise the information by selecting the main points and reporting the main features, and make comparisons where relevant.

Write at least 150 words.

Average number of daily journeys taken (by transport type) in 1985 and 2015

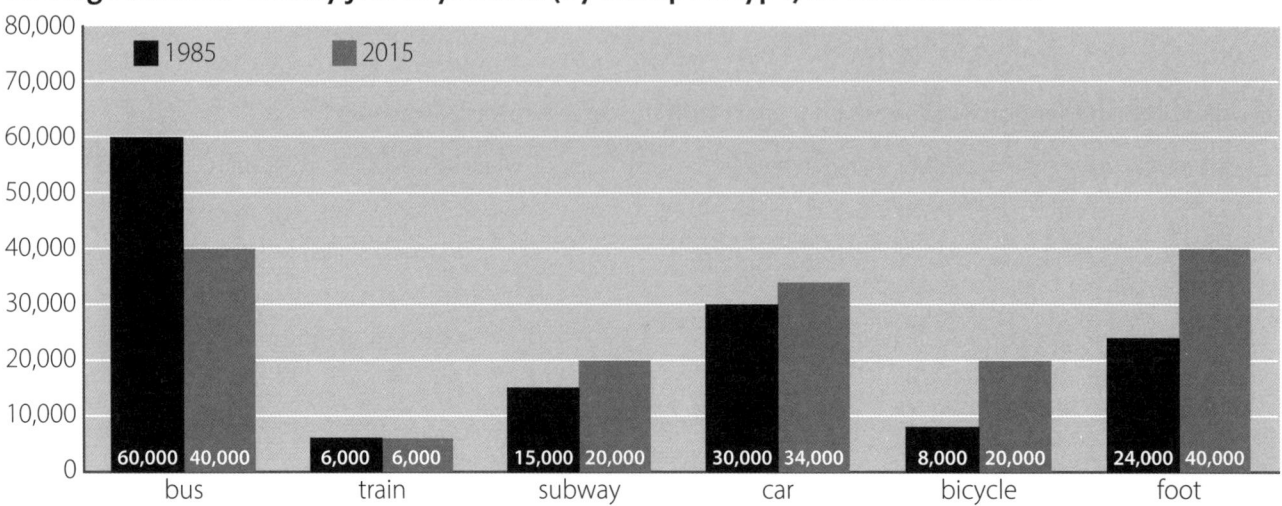

Too many cars

1a **Work in pairs. Look at the photo and discuss the questions.**

a) What problem does it show? b) What do you know about this problem? c) What can be done to solve it?

1b **Do you agree or disagree with the statements? Discuss your ideas.**

- Governments should spend more money on public transport.

- People use cars much more than in the past.

- Cars should be banned from city centres.

- There will be driverless cars in the future.

> **Exam tip**
>
> In IELTS Writing Task 2, you should try to use a range of different grammar to talk about the past, present and future. What grammar did you use to discuss the statements above?

2a **Match the sentences (1–6) from a Task 2 essay with the grammar functions (a–f).**

> Cars should be banned from city centres. To what extent do you agree or disagree with this statement?

1) 50 years ago, most people in my country did not have a car. ...._b_....

2) Trains can be an enjoyable way to travel. ....

3) In the future, many cities will be even bigger than than are today. ....

4) In my country, the government has built a lot of new roads in the last five years. ....

5) Many cities are becoming more polluted. ....

6) Driverless cars may become much more popular. ....

a) talking about the future

b) talking about the past

c) talking about things which are changing now

d) talking about things which have changed recently

e) talking about something which is sometimes true

f) talking about something which is possible

2b **Look at the sentences in exercise 2a again. Which sentences use a modal verb to talk about present or future possibility?**

3a Work in pairs. Complete the Task 2 essay with the correct form of the words in brackets, so that it uses a range of grammar. Add modal verbs where appropriate.

> Governments should stop building new roads and should spend more money on railways instead. To what extent do you agree or disagree with this statement?

*The number of cars **(1)** is increasing .... (increase) around the world. In some countries, the government **(2)** .... (build) many more roads for these extra cars. In this essay I will discuss whether this should stop, and governments should spend the money on improving railways instead.*

*Trains have many benefits in comparison with cars. They cause less pollution and they do not cause traffic jams. Although there **(3)** .... (be) some train accidents, trains are much safer than cars. However, train travel **(4)** .... (be) slower and more inconvenient than travelling by car. Trains **(5)** .... (be) old and crowded. In the past, people **(6)** .... (not expect) to get from one place to another quickly and comfortably, but now they do.*

*Spending a lot of money on improving railways **(7)** .... (help) to make them more attractive, and then more people **(8)** .... (want) to use them. However, this **(9)** .... (cause) political problems. It **(10)** .... (be) difficult for a government to explain to people that railways are more important than roads. People love the freedom of travelling by car. Of course, nobody likes traffic jams, and many people think that building more roads **(11)** .... (end) traffic jams. Some people say that if the government builds more roads, the traffic **(12)** .... (increase) to fill those roads. However, many people **(13)** .... (ask) their government to build more roads.*

*In conclusion, I believe that governments around the world should stop building roads and should start spending a lot more money on railways. However, I believe that this **(14)** .... (not happen) for political reasons.*

3b Work with another pair. Compare your versions. Did you use the same grammar and modal verbs? if your choice are different, are they still correct?

4 Write an answer to the Task 2 question. Try to use a range of grammar.

EXAM TASK: Writing (Task 2)

Planes cause pollution which contributes to global warming. There should be a high tax on plane tickets to reduce the amount of air travel. To what extent do you agree or disagree with this statement?

Give reasons for your answer and include any relevant examples from your own knowledge or experience.

Write at least 250 words.

Improve your work!

1 **Work in pairs. Find and correct the punctuation and spelling errors in the extract from a Task 1 essay.**

> The graphs show the average audience share for terrestrial television channels in a European country.
>
> Summarise the information by selecting the main points and reporting the main features, and make comparisons where relevant.
>
> Write at least 150 words.

the two pie charts show the average audeince shares for the terrestrial chanels of a Europan country in 1999 and 2009

in 1999, there were six chanels. Channel 1 had the largest proprtion, at 40% next were Channels 2 and 3 with 14% and 25%. Sport TV had a shar of 11%, while Art Media's share was just over half that figur. News Today had the smallest audience share at 4%

Ten years leter, there were three new channls. Films Plus had the largest audienc share with 15%. Comedy Station, and Kids TV had 9% and 4%. The declin was not evenly spred among the other channels. News Today's share did not chang, and Sport TV's share went down by just one percent. In contrast, Channels 1 to 3 all lost a larg propurtion of there adience. Channel 1's share droped to 26%, Channel 2's to 10%, and Channel 3's to 19%. The bigest drop was Art media, which lost half its audience share.

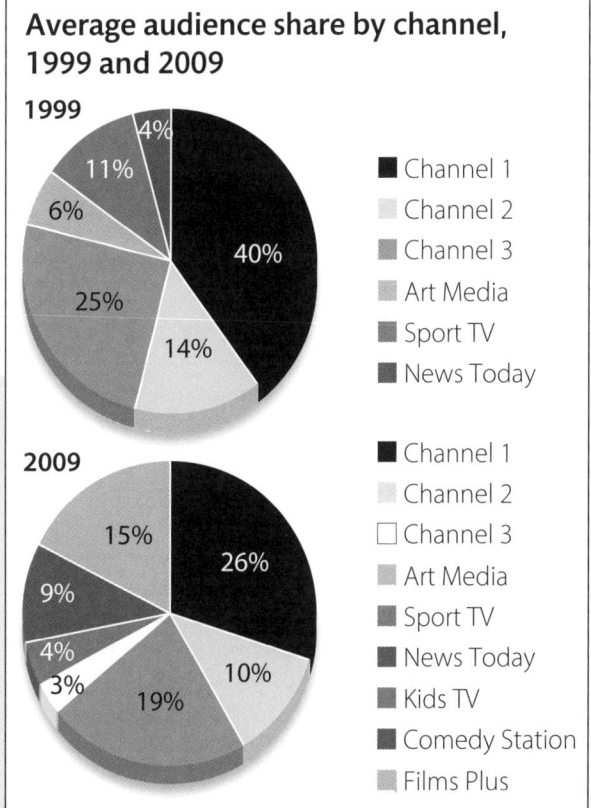

Average audience share by channel, 1999 and 2009

1999

- ■ Channel 1
- ▢ Channel 2
- ▨ Channel 3
- ▨ Art Media
- ▨ Sport TV
- ■ News Today

2009

- ■ Channel 1
- ▢ Channel 2
- ▢ Channel 3
- ▨ Art Media
- ▨ Sport TV
- ■ News Today
- ▨ Kids TV
- ■ Comedy Station
- ▨ Films Plus

Exam tip

Always check your work for spelling, punctuation and grammar mistakes. You are allowed to make corrections in the IELTS Writing test, but they must be clear and easy to read. Correcting errors may make a big difference to your score.

2 **Work in pairs. Correct the underlined grammar mistakes in the Task 2 essay.**

> Governments should spend money on supporting arts such as the theatre, live music and independent film-making. To what extent do you agree with this statement?
>
> Give reasons for your answer and include any relevant examples from your own knowledge or experience.
>
> Write at least 250 words.

*In many countries, **(1)** <u>governments gives</u> some money to support the theatre, live music and independent film makers. In this essay, I will discuss if I think **(2)** <u>this a good way</u> to spend taxpayer's money.*

*Many of the arts which benefit from government money have **(3)** <u>very small audience</u>. For example, opera houses **(4)** <u>can to hold</u> only **(5)** <u>few hundreds of people</u> and some independent films **(6)** <u>are only see</u> by a few thousand people. The money they receive **(7)** <u>come</u> from taxpayers **(8)** <u>who they have worked hard</u> to earn that money. However, the majority of those taxpayers **(9)** <u>never will see</u> the operas, independent films, etc. which **(10)** <u>they have pay</u> to support. I do not believe this is fair. It would be **(11)** <u>better spend</u> the money on **(12)** <u>thing</u> which benefit a larger number of people.*

3   Work in pairs. Look at the example Task 2 essay. Tick the things the writer does or does not do.

	yes	no
uses paragraphs		✓
repeats words or ideas too many times		
uses the same words as the task question		
always writes in an academic style		
sometimes uses complex sentences		
uses linking words		
always stays on the topic of the question		
makes clear arguments and answers the question well		
writes 250 words		

EXAM TASK: Writing (Task 2)

People are increasingly watching less television at the time it is broadcast, and watching 'on demand' TV via the internet. Is this a positive or a negative development?

Give reasons for your answer and include any relevant examples from your own knowledge or experience.

Write at least 250 words.

People are increasingly watching less television and watching it via the internet. In this essay I will discuss whether this is a positive or a negative development. However, the best TV shows are on the internet, and I love them! I don't like paying for TV shows. It seems just another way for media companies to get more money from people. In my country, there are around 50 TV channels to choose from. Most on demand TV shows are American, and most of these shows are made in America. Many American TV shows are excellent. All my favourite shows are American. I don't like watching shows which are made in my country, because they aren't so interesting. However, I believe that it is important that we try to keep our national TV shows, which is a part of our culture. It is a valuable thing for all of us. In conclusion, I believe that 'on demand' TV shows are good, because you can watch TV shows when you want to.

4   Write your essay for the Task 2 question in exercise 3.

IELTS WRITING TASK 1

You should spend about 20 minutes on this task.

The charts below show the number of visitors to a town in the UK from three different countries and the total number of overseas visitors to the UK from 2011 to 2015.

Summarise the information by selecting and reporting the main features, and make comparisons where relevant.

Write at least 150 words.

Number of visits to a town in the UK by country

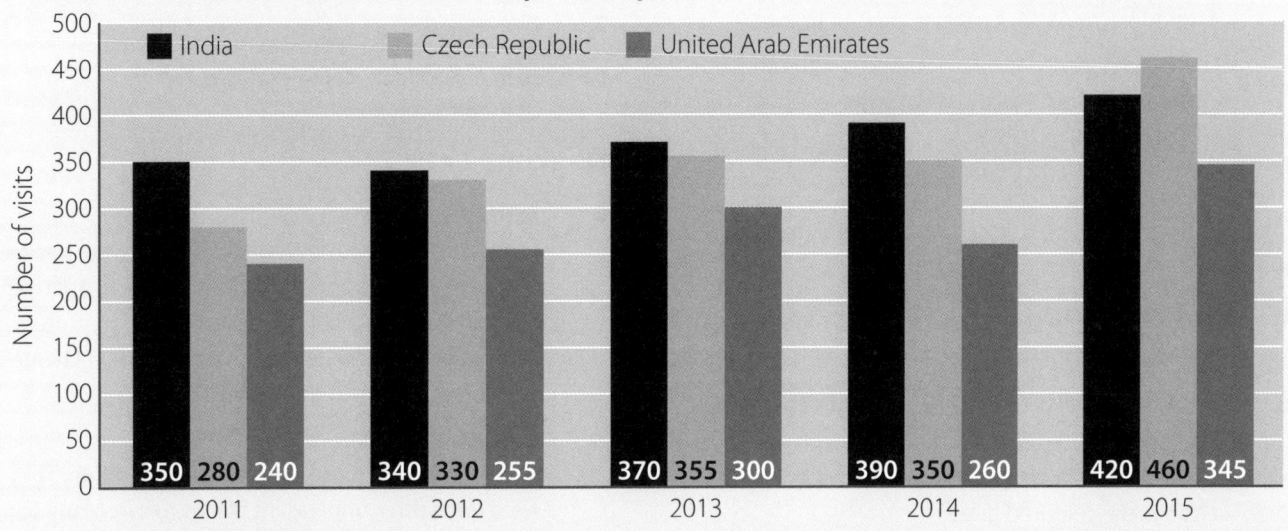

Total visits to the town from all overseas countries

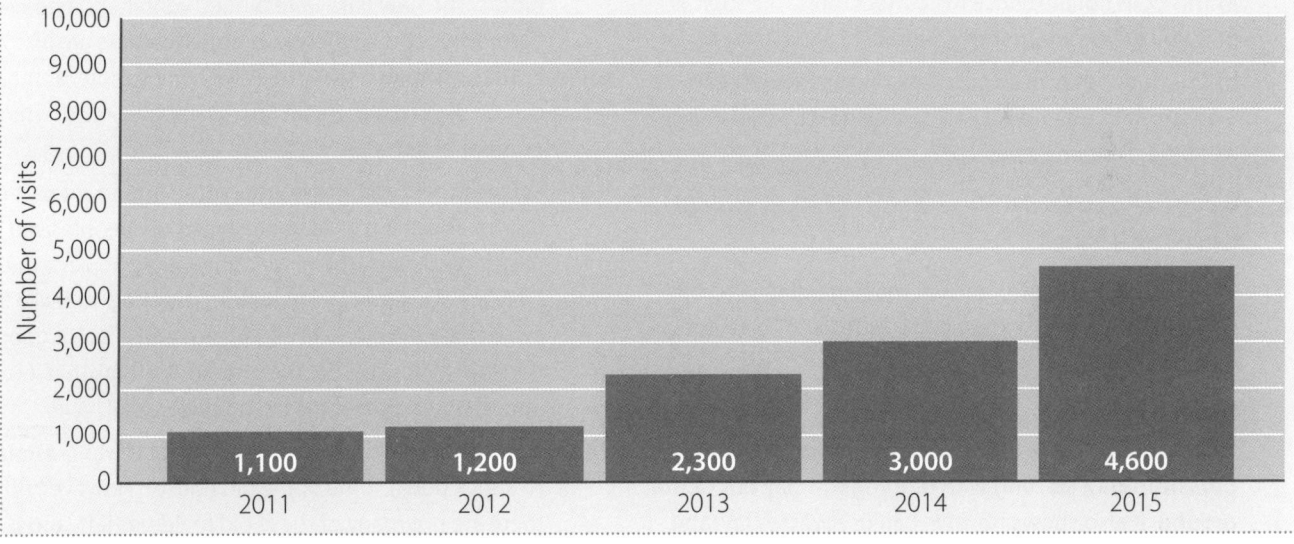

IELTS WRITING TASK 2

You should spend about 40 minutes on this task.

Write about the following topic:

These days, many people rely on their mobile phones for different things, such as communicating with friends, getting news or taking photos. Is this a positive or a negative development?

Give reasons for your answer and include any relevant examples from your own knowledge or experience.

Write at least 250 words.

Answers

Getting started (pages 6–8)

Exam tip capital letters 10 (there are 5 capital letters in IELTS), full stops 3, commas 1, question marks 1

2 **2** a **3** d **4** e **5** b

3b **a)** In the IELTS Writing test, you will see a picture (a diagram, a graph or a table). You need to describe the data in the picture. You have to report the important information. You do not need to give an opinion.

b) You have to write at least 150 words. You can write more than this, but you must not write less than this.

c) You only have about 20 minutes to understand the picture and write your description. You cannot afford to waste any time.

4a B

4b **b** pot **c** clay **d** firing **e** glaze **f** waste **g** minerals **h** pottery **i** pug mill

5a This diagram shows the process of making handmade pots from clay, starting with digging the clay out of the ground. It also shows how we can use waste clay, and how we can make coloured glaze.

5b A

6 **a)** This does not introduce the correct topic. The topic is how you make pots, not why people make pots by hand.

b) This does not give an overview of what the diagram is about. In Writing Task 1, we usually start by explaining what the diagram shows.

7a **b** pug mill **c** pottery **d** Waste **e** pug mill **f** kiln **g** glaze **h** minerals **j** firing

7b C We usually put these words at the beginning of a sentence. They start with a capital letter, and there is a comma after them.

8 **Sample answer**
This diagram shows the process of making handmade pots from clay, starting with digging the clay out of the ground. It also shows how we can use waste clay, and how we can make coloured glaze.

First, someone digs the clay from the ground. Next, the pieces of clay go into a pug mill, so that the clay can be usable. After that, the usable clay goes into a pottery, and someone makes it into pots.

The waste clay from this process can go into water. Then, the waste clay goes back into the pug mill, which turns it back into usable clay.

When the pots have been made, they go into a kiln for the first firing. After the first firing, we can apply coloured glaze to them. This glaze is made by mixing coloured minerals with clear glaze. Next, the pots

return to the kiln for the second firing. Finally, the pots are ready, and can go on sale in shops.

What's the topic? (pages 9–11)

2b **2)** question **3)** opinion **4)** 250 **5)** 60

3 **b)** more than one **c)** is **d)** one clear topic **e)** first

5 **b)** 4 **c)** 3 **d)** 1

6a **b)** In my opinion **c)** For example, **d)** In this essay, I will

6b **2** d **3** a **4** b

8 **Sample answer**
In my country, thousands of old houses were destroyed because people wanted to build and live in apartment blocks. However, most people now want to protect the old houses we have left. Some people are in favour of this and some are not. In this essay, I will discuss reasons for and against protecting old houses.

Many of the old houses were in bad condition. They were unhealthy, unpleasant places to live. Many of them were too small and did not have proper kitchens and bathrooms. People wanted to move to new apartment blocks. The new flats were bigger, lighter and had good bathrooms and kitchens. Apartment blocks are also a better way to use space in a city. For example, a small area can be big enough for an apartment block with a large number of flats.

On the other hand, old houses are an important part of our history. They help us to understand how people lived in the past. If we destroy them, we cannot easily replace them. They are also attractive to look at. They help to make life in a city a more pleasant experience and it is also good for the tourist industry. For these reasons, I think that it is very important to protect the old houses we still have.

In conclusion, I believe that in the past it was reasonable to knock down some of the old houses. However, now there are not many of these old buildings left, and it is important to protect them.

Academic subjects (pages 12–13)

1b **Possible answers**
arts and humanities: art, design, literature
professional degrees: business, law
social sciences: psychology, sociology
sciences: chemistry, physics, biology

2 B is the best overview, because it summarises all the data that we can see, in a short and easy way. There is no need to give an opinion in IELTS Writing Task 1.

3b **b)** 1,550 **c)** 970 **d)**1990 **e)** 1,040 **f)** 90 **g)** 2,000

4 **b)** 1 **c)** 4 **d)** 3

5 **went up:** increased, rose
went down: decreased, fell

6 **Sample answer**
For these two years, the number of children learning French decreased to 39%. The number learning German only fell slightly, to 12%. The number learning Spanish only doubled. Children who learned another foreign language rose significantly, from 2% to 15%. The number of children learning two or more languages also increased significantly, up to 28%. In 1975, 8% of 12 year olds were not learning any language, but this dropped to 0% in 2015.

Education issues (pages 14–15)

2 **2** b **3** a

3a **b)** 1 **c)** 4 **d)** 3

3b The notes are not full sentences, and don't have normal punctuation. When you write notes, you don't need to write correctly, because you are only writing for yourself. You are writing ideas down quickly, to help you plan your real essay.

3c **a)** The ideas are the same, but they are written in full sentences.

4 **Sample answer**
In my country, most children do not start learning a foreign language until they are 9 or 10. In my opinion, it would be better to start earlier, but there are some practical reasons why this is not possible.

Very young children are much quicker at learning languages. Generally speaking, they do not have to work very hard to learn the new language. Just hearing it around them is often enough for them to learn it quickly and well. If all children began learning a second language as soon as they started school, then by the time they were 9 or 10, many of them would be able to speak it to an advanced level. Instead, most children do not start learning until they are 9, and never reach a very high level.

However, I can see two reasons not to start until later. Firstly, very young children might become confused between the two languages, and might start mixing their native language with the foreign language. This could especially be a problem when the two languages have different alphabets. Secondly, in my country there is already a shortage of language teachers in schools. I think it would be very difficult to find enough teachers to start giving language lessons to very young children.

In conclusion, I believe that it would be good for children to start learning foreign languages at a younger age, but there might be problems if the children do not get enough help, or have good teachers.

Property prices (pages 16–17)

1a **b)** semi-detached houses **c)** terraced houses
d) flats / apartments

Exam tip Although the information is about the past, the chart, graph or table exists in the present.

2 Introduction c is the best. It paraphrases the question and it gives a general description of the information. a and b miss some important information and include some irrelevant information, which isn't needed.

3a **b)** gives **c)** illustrates **d)** provides

3b It means *the graph*. We can use it to avoid repeating the same words.

4 **Sample answer**
The graph gives information about how much money young people aged 20–35 spent from 1975 to 2015. It shows the percentage of their income they spent on rent, food and household bills.

The best place to live (pages 18–19)

1 **2** d **3** e/a/b **4** b **5** c

1c **b** factories
c a town or city with lots of people
d just outside a city centre
e the people you live next to

Exam tip **b)** You should never repeat exactly the same words or phrases that are in an IELTS question. This might stop you getting a higher score.

2a **2** city centres **3** advantages **4** disadvantages

2b **2** urban areas
3 factories and warehouses
4 advantages
5 disadvantages
6 change

3b **Sample answers**
a) In some people's opinion, we should build new houses in rural areas, because there is space there. Others think that we should build new houses in old industrial areas. In this essay, I will discuss both points of view and give my own opinion.

b) In some cities, the cost of housing is now so high that some workers cannot afford to live near the places where they work. In this essay, I will discuss the causes of this problem and what people can do to solve it.

c) In some countries, it is usual for young people to share houses with each other. In other countries, young people usually live with their parents until they get married. In this essay, I will discuss the advantages and disadvantages of sharing a house with people of your own age.

Sporting activities (pages 20–21)

1b   **1 b / c** line graphs and bar charts are good for showing trends over time

2 b / c line graphs and bar charts are good for showing trends over time

3 a pie charts are good for showing percentages

4 d process diagrams are good for showing how something happens

2   percentage

3b   **2** 1% **3** 7% **4** 3% **5** youth sports clubs **6** 41% **7** 19% **8** 2004 **9** 39% **10** 2014

4   **Sample answer**

The two pie charts show the sports activities which were selected by students at an American high school in 2003 and 2013.

The most popular sport in both years was football, but the percentage of students choosing this sport fell from 44% to 37%. The second most popular sport in both years was basketball, but the number choosing this sport also fell. In 2003 the figure was 28%, and by 2013 it had fallen to 22%. The third and final decline was in the share of students who chose tennis. This proportion fell from 9% to 6%.

The biggest increase was in the proportion choosing volleyball. This almost doubled from 12% in 2003 to 23% in 2013. The proportion of students choosing other sports rose by just 1% to 5% in 2013. There was a larger increase in the percentage of students who did no sports. This more than doubled, rising from 3% to 7%.

Why do we do sport? (pages 22–23)

2   **a)** True. You need to introduce the topic, and say what you are going to write about.

b) False. It is important to write in paragraphs, if you want to get a good score: an introduction, two main paragraphs, and a conclusion. (Two main paragraphs is common, but more than two is acceptable.)

c) False. The IELTS Writing test tests whether you can argue different points of view.

d) True. The conclusion summarises all the arguments, and ends with your opinion.

3a   Conclusion **b)** – this is the best. The writer summarises the arguments in the main paragraphs, chooses one view and explains why.

3b   **1** c **2** a

4   **2** Say which argument you agree with most.

3 Justify your opinion.

5a   **a)** Some people believe computer games are similar to sports, and are a useful way to spend time. How much do you agree or disagree with this?

b) Some people believe that it is useful to encourage students to do team sports in school. Other people believe that there may be disadvantages. Discuss both views and decide whether the advantages outweigh the disadvantages.

5b   **but:** although, however **because:** as

6b   **Sample answers**

In conclusion, although it is true that the costs of major international sporting events can be very high, they can also have some important benefits for international relations. My opinion is that they are not a waste of money. If they can help to promote world peace, then no price is too high to pay.

In conclusion, large sporting events such as the Olympic Games have benefits for international relations. However, the costs have become far too high. I believe that much less money should be spent on these events. The money saved could be used to help solve problems around the world.

Work and money (pages 24–25)

1b   **b)** shop assistant **c)** builder **d)** tour guide **e)** accountant **f)** farmer

2a   **b)** We don't need to add up the numbers exactly to see that the total number of people working in each industry is similar, but not exactly the same, in most cases.

2b   **2** about/approximately/around

3 just

4 about/approximately/around/nearly

5 about/approximately/around

6 under

7 just

8 about/approximately/around

Exam tip b)

2c   **Sample answer**

France has the most people working in the tourism industry at nearly 3.5 million. Italy and Spain both have approximately 3 million and Germany has the fewest at just under 2 million.

In the financial services industry, Spain has the most workers at approximately 2.2 million. France and Germany both have between 1.5 and 2 million, while Italy has just under 1 million.

France and Italy both have around half a million workers in agriculture, while Spain and Germany both have about a quarter of a million.

3   **a)** lawyer, secretary

b) doctor, accountant, journalist, nurse **c)** teacher

d) secretary, nurse

4a **Sample answer**

The table shows the average annual salaries in euros for men and women in nine different professions. It also shows the average pay for all occupations for both men and women.

In some of the professions listed in the table, men earn a lot more than women. For example, male company directors earn nearly €30,000 more and male lawyers earn around €10,000 more. In other professions, the difference is smaller, or there is no real difference. Male doctors, accountants, and journalists earn only slightly more than women.

Male and female teachers earn exactly the same amount of money. Women earn more than men in only two of the professions listed: nurses and secretaries.

In conclusion, the table shows that men usually earn more than women for doing the same jobs. The average pay for women is approximately €28,000, which is around €3,000 less than the average annual salary for men.

A fair day's work (pages 26–27)

1b The grammar and vocabulary are fine. However, this introduction is not relevant to the question. It is talking about a different topic.

1c Sentences b and f should not be included. The question is about salaries for men and women, not about salaries for different occupations.

Exam tip Idea **c)** is not correct. You get marks for the quality of your writing, not for how many ideas you include. However, you should include enough ideas to answer the question.

3b **Sample answer**

People have different reasons for choosing a job. Some are looking for job satisfaction, while others want to earn a lot of money. In this essay I will discuss both points of view, and I will give my own opinion.

If a person's job has high job satisfaction, that person will probably enjoy his or her time at work more. Unfortunately, many jobs with high levels of job satisfaction are not well paid. For example, many artists, musicians and writers earn very little. Jobs which mean helping other people, such as nursing and teaching, also tend to have high job satisfaction but again are not very well paid. For people who choose these occupations, their dreams of helping other people are probably more important than the amount of money they earn.

In contrast, other people choose jobs because of the amount of money they will earn. For example, in my country, university subjects like law or economics are popular. This is because people believe that they will get a good job if they study these subjects. However, this does not mean that they love law or economics. They might prefer to study art or music, but know that this will not lead to a well paid career.

In my opinion, it is difficult to find a job which pays well, and also makes you happy. However, you spend a very large amount of your life at work, so it is important to do something that you enjoy, otherwise, your days will be very depressing. In the end, happiness is more important than making money.

Problems and their causes (pages 28–29)

Exam tip Factories make pollution. This causes acid rain. Because of this, trees and plants die.

2a **2** d **3** a **4** c **5** h **6** e **7** f **8** g

2b **Process 1**

2 The sea melts the glacier

3 The glacier breaks up into icebergs

4 The glacier flows into the sea faster

5 The sea level rises

Process 2

1 The top of the glacier melts

2 The meltwater goes down through the glacier

3 The meltwater lubricates the flow of the glacier

4 The glacier flows into the sea faster

5 The sea level rises

2c a

2d **2** icebergs **3** causes **4** Because **5** snow **6** lubricates **7** result **8** cause

3 **Sample answer**

The diagram shows the effects of acid rain on the water in lakes and rivers. It shows a power station, a lake, a road with some vehicles and some dead trees.

Acidic gases from power stations, cars and lorries rise up into the atmosphere. They combine with water in the atmosphere and come back down to the ground in the form of acid rain. This acid rain enters rivers, and these rivers flow into lakes. Because of this acid in rivers and lakes, some plants and animals in the water die, but some survive. The result of this is that some plants survive and take over.

The acid rain kills plants on land too. This means that they die, and their roots no longer hold the topsoil in place. This causes the topsoil to go into lakes and rivers. This results in more pollution and rising acidity in the water.

Looking after the planet (page 30–31)

Exam tip It is better if each paragraph has one clear focus. This shows that you can organise your ideas clearly, and makes it easy for the reader to follow them.

2 There are lots of good ideas, but there is no clear argument. The paragraph keeps switching from one topic/view to another. This makes it more difficult to read and understand what the writer wants to say.

3c **b** 3 **c** 1

4a **Sample answer**
On the other hand, a lot of work to protect animals has been successful. For example, there are several species, like pandas or leopards, which are only here now because they are protected. Without any protection, many of our most famous animals would probably be extinct. When an animal is extinct, it is gone forever. We need to spend money protecting our natural world, because humans cannot live in a world without animals, forests, or clean seas.

5 The problem is that it is too strong. The writer is exaggerating. Using language like *everybody*, *nobody* and *the worst* is not usual in academic writing. It is not really possible to say what 'everybody' or 'nobody' will think or do.

6b **Sample answer**
Humans have used animals for a very long time. One of the main uses of animals is for food. We also use animals to make clothes. In many countries, animals like dogs, horses and elephants are used for work. In science, we use animals to test our medicines, and things like shampoo. In this essay, I will give the arguments for and against using animals, and give my own opinion.

There are many reasons why humans should not use animals. For example, many people think that it is cruel to use animals for their meat, or for experiments. There are many alternatives to using animals. We could eat mostly vegetables and fruit. Doing this would help the environment. Also, we don't need to use animals for work nowadays, because we have machines to do these jobs.

However, some people think that it is necessary to use animals. For example, meat is an important source of food for most people around the world. Also, without animals such as mice, we could not do important scientific experiments which help humans develop their knowledge. Using animals can help save lives, and stop people from being hungry.

In conclusion, there are advantages and disadvantages to using animals. Certainly, animals have helped human society to become advanced. In my opinion, humans need to think about whether they need to use animals so much. As our society and technology becomes more advanced, we should use our knowledge to find alternatives to using animals, and leave animals in the natural world, where they belong.

The circle of life (page 32–34)

1a The photos show a frog, a cicada and a salmon.

2 **2** first **3** Eventually **4** point **5** Finally

3 **2** and **3** After this **4** At this point **5** Eventually **6** Then **7** after **8** and **9** and then

5 **Sample answer**
The diagram shows the life cycle of the salmon. It is divided into ~~seven~~ _{six} main stages.

The salmon lay their eggs at the bottom of a river, in the reeds and gravel. Later, in the spring, the eggs hatch, and the baby salmon, which are called smolts, emerge from the eggs. At first, these smolts are tiny but they start to grow in the river. After two to four years they have grown much bigger, and then they start to swim down the river towards the sea. They spend one to four years in the sea, and then they return to same river where they were born. Next, they swim up this river. At this point, they start to change shape. Eventually, they arrive back at the part of the river where they were born. Finally, the females lay their eggs at the bottom of the river, and the cycle begins again.

Solving the problem (pages 35–36)

2a **causes** a and b **solutions** c and d

2b **2** As a result **3** the most common reason for **4** a simple solution to this problem **5** This would mean that **6** is a result of

4 **Sample answer**
In some countries, it is more common nowadays to see overweight children. This is very bad for their health, when they become adults. In this essay, I will discuss some of the reasons for this problem, and some possible solutions.

A major cause of being overweight is eating the wrong kind of food. Children love fast food, snacks and sweets, so when they have a choice of what to eat, they often choose to eat these things. Another reason for this problem is advertising. Advertisers are very good at making unhealthy foods attractive to children. The children then ask their parents to buy these foods. The food the parents eat is also a reason for this problem. In many homes, children eat the same food as their parents.

A simple solution is not to put unhealthy food in front of children. For example, shops and fast food restaurants should not put sweets or sugary drinks in places where children can easily see them. Another possible solution is to ban companies from advertising unhealthy foods, especially to children. Educating people about the dangers of eating unhealthy food could also help to solve this problem. If more adults understand the dangers of eating a lot of unhealthy food, then maybe fewer parents would give unhealthy food to their children.

In conclusion, the problem of children being overweight is caused by unhealthy food being too easy to buy. The solution is to find ways to keep children away from unhealthy food so that they eat healthy food instead.

How was it made? (pages 37–39)

2 **b)** is melted, is turned **c)** is folded, is changed
 d) was built **e)** were used

3a **2** a **3** d **4** b **5** f **6** e

3b **2** are heated **3** are put **4** are filled **5** are cooled
 6 are removed **7** are sent **8** are put **9** are loaded
 10 are taken

4 **2** c **3** a **4** b **5** d

5 **Sample answer**
The diagram shows how cement is made. It is divided into several main stages.
First, limestone is taken from a quarry. Then, the limestone is taken to the cement factory. Trucks are used for this. The limestone arrives at the factory and the rocks are crushed into small pieces. After that, these small pieces are crushed into even smaller pieces. This process produces very small pieces of limestone. Eventually, this is mixed with sand and clay.
This mixture is put into a preheater, and from there it is put in a kiln. The kiln is very hot. The mixture is heated to 1,400 °C. Then the mixture is cooled. After this, the mixture goes through a final grinding mill. It is ground one more time. Finally, the finished cement is delivered to customers.

Online shopping (pages 40–41)

Exam tip It means 'are there more advantages than disadvantages'.

2c **b** 2 **c** 1 **d** 7 **e** 4 **f** 3 **g** 6

3c **Sample answer**
Buying things online has become a very common way to shop. In this essay, I will discuss the advantages and disadvantages of online shopping, and give my opinion about whether or not the advantages outweigh the disadvantages.

The main advantage of online shopping for many people is that it is quick and easy. Clicking 'buy' is obviously much faster than travelling to a shop and walking around it. Also, online shopping often has more choice than a physical shop. You can buy exactly want you want, instead of the only things that the shop has. A third advantage is price. Buying things online is sometimes cheaper than buying them in a physical shop.

The popularity of online shopping has made it difficult for some shops to survive, and many have closed down. Interesting shops are part of the character of a town or city, and it can spoil a town or city if many of the shops have disappeared. Visiting a shop is a way to meet other people, and to be part of a community. In a shop, you might meet a friend or neighbour and have a conversation. Obviously, this does not happen when you shop alone on the internet.

In conclusion, shopping online is a convenient and efficient way to shop. The disadvantages are that physical shops are closing, and people are spending less time being a part of their local community. However, in my opinion, the advantages of online shopping outweigh the disadvantages. There are other ways to be part of the local community.

This place has really changed! (pages 42–44)

2b **b)** False **c)** True **d)** True **e)** True **f)** False

3a **b)** goes **c)** have disappeared, **d)** have grown **e)** is

3b **b)** have been cut down **c)** has been built

4 **a)** It has been replaced with a cycle track and a footpath, the car park has been converted into a park, in the ~~middle~~ south of the park, there is now a boating lake.

 b) The pier ~~was~~ has been demolished, there ~~is~~ was a road, an art gallery has been built

 c) There is a small picture of a bicycle on the cycle track and a small picture of a person on the footpath.

5 The two maps show a lake as it was in 2014, and as it is now, after it has been developed as a place for tourists.

In 2014 there was a car park to the west of the lake, and there was an old factory to the north. There were no other buildings. After the redevelopment of this area, the car park is now bigger, and the old factory has been changed into a study centre. To the south and east of the lake, several new buildings have been built. To the east, there is now a reception building and several smaller buildings for accommodation. To the south of the lake, a restaurant has been built. There is now a pier at the south end of the lake and a bridge has been built across the lake in the north part. A footpath now goes all the way around the lake.

The tourist dollar (pages 45–46)

2a **b)** However **c)** Although/While **d)** and **e)** also
 f) Also/In addition **g)** so **h)** Therefore **i)** Because
 j) because

3 **Sample answer**
Tourism is a very important industry all over the world, and a holiday is the best part of the year for many people. However, tourism often does not benefit local communities as much as it could.

While tourism creates many jobs, most of these jobs are not well paid. In addition, many jobs in tourism are only for the summer season. Although these jobs are better than no job, they often do not bring much money to local people.

Tourists spend a lot of money, <u>so</u> people think that tourism benefits local businesses. <u>However</u>, a lot of the money tourists spend does not actually benefit local businesses, <u>because</u> it goes to big companies who own most of the shops, hotels and restaurants. Some of the money tourists spend may not even benefit the country they are visiting, <u>because</u> it goes to international companies. <u>While</u> some tourists try to spend money with small local businesses, many are not aware of this problem.

<u>Although</u> many tourists respect local customs and behave in a responsible way, some do not. Some tourists do not learn about local customs before they visit a country, <u>therefore</u> they do not know what will upset local people. While this may not seem very important, tourists' behaviour can make local people unhappy.

In conclusion, I agree that tourism does not always benefit local people. The big companies which make money from tourism should pay their workers more <u>and</u> tourists should try to spend more money with local businesses. <u>In addition</u>, tourists should have more respect for local customs.

The news today (pages 47–48)

2a   **a)** The table shows how many people read a national newspaper in 2000 and 2015. The table gives information for five different age groups.
b) There are fewer younger readers in 2015 than in 2000.
c) There are more older readers in 2015 than in 2000.
d) There are slightly fewer readers in 2015, in total.

2b   **2** data **3** age groups **4** the years **5** total number of

3a   It repeats *went down* and *went up* too many times.

4a   **by a lot:** dramatically, significantly, considerably
by a little: slightly

5   **2** dramatic fall **3** decreased significantly
4 dropped slightly **5** increased slightly
6 considerable rise

6   **Sample answer**
The table shows the average number of visitors to a news website each week for the years 2006 and 2016, listed by annual income. It also shows the total number of visitors in those years.

The number of visitors with incomes below €15,000 nearly doubled from 34,000 in 2006 to 67,000 in 2016. The number of visitors with incomes of €15,000 to just below €30,000 rose even more significantly from 45,000 to just over 100,000. This was the most dramatic increase. The number of visitors with incomes between €30,000 and €44,999 rose only slightly, increasing from 50,000 to 52,000. In contrast, the number of visitors with incomes from €45,000 to €59,999 and over €60,000 decreased

significantly, falling from 42,000 to 15,000 and 34,000 to just 9,000 respectively. The total number of visitors rose from just over 205,000 to 244,000.

In conclusion, the figures show that visitors with lower incomes increased, while visitors with higher incomes decreased. There was an increase in the total number of visitors.

Old and new media (pages 49–50)

2   **1** Suitable. You can admit that the topic is outside your own experience.
2 Not suitable. Too much personal experience, and too informal.
3 Suitable. This example of personal experience could help to support an argument.
4 Not suitable. You must try to answer the question, even if you know very little about the topic.
5 Not suitable. Too much specialised knowledge which is not relevant to supporting an argument.
6 Suitable. This piece of knowledge could help to support an argument.

4   **Sample answer**
It is becoming more and more difficult for newspapers to compete with news from websites, and sales of many newspapers are going down. In this essay, I will discuss whether I think this is a positive or a negative development.

Getting news from the internet has many advantages over buying a newspaper. Most news websites are free. You can check the news whenever you want, quickly and easily. You can do it on a smartphone or a tablet or a laptop computer. Another benefit is that the news is updated very quickly on websites, while news in a printed newspaper may be two or three days old. This makes online news very attractive. In my county, printed newspapers are still popular with older people, but people of my age do not buy them very often. I check the news online every day, but I cannot remember the last time I bought a printed newspaper.

However, I sometimes read printed newspapers when I visit my parents. The articles tend to be longer, and they cover the topic in more detail. I also read longer articles which I would probably not take the time to read online. In addition, I have noticed that there seems to be more serious journalism in newspapers than there is online.

Personally, I still prefer to get news from the internet, but I think it would be bad if newspapers disappeared. In some ways, they are better than online news.

Changing cities (pages 51–52)

2 **2** C **3** F **4** A **5** D **6** E

3a

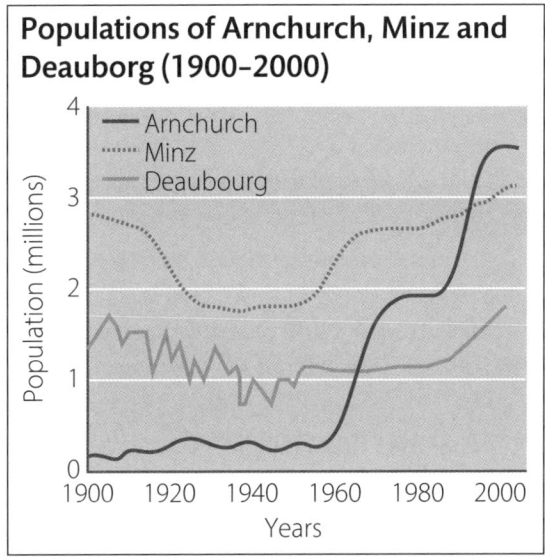

Populations of Arnchurch, Minz and Deauborg (1900–2000)

3b just under 3 million, around 2 million, fairly level, about 3 million, less than a quarter of a million, fairly level, almost 2 million, about 2 million, just below 4 million

4 **Sample answer**

The chart shows population changes in three European cities over the last century.

In 1900, Barnheim had a population of around 200,000. This increased dramatically until 1910. Then it levelled off at around 2 million. It started to rise again in the 1960s. It continued to rise until the early 1980s, then it levelled off and by 2000 it was around 4 million.

Astbury's population was about 700,000 in 1900. It rose gradually until about 1950, when it reached around 1.5 million. Then it started to fluctuate, although in general in went up. By 2000 the population was approximately 2 million.

The population of Couville was around 1.3 million at the beginning of the century. It gradually decreased to less than half a million in the 1950s. It started to rise in around 1970, and reached approximately 1.5 million at the end of the 1980s. Then it started to go down again, and by the end of the century it had fallen to just under a million.

Crowded cities (page 53–54)

Exam tip a) informal **b)** neutral

2 **b)** S **c)** NS **d)** S **e)** NS **f)** NS **g)** NS

3 **a)** I will tell you about the causes of this problem and some possible solutions.
b) Life is incredibly stressful for everybody who lives in a city.
c) They cannot easily leave their jobs and the places where they live.
d) Cities are so strange.
e) Maybe people are travelling a lot, but I don't know where.

4a **Sample answer**

Many cities are increasing in in size, and this trend is expected to continue in the future. In this essay I will discuss whether or not I see this as a positive or a negative development.

I believe that one of the main causes of cities increasing in size is people moving there from the surrounding areas. Living in cites has many obvious benefits in comparison with living in the countryside. There tend to be better job opportunities and more leisure and entertainment facilities. It is easy to see why so many people decide to move to cities.

However, city life has several negative sides too. Cities can be stressful places to live, and many cities are very polluted. In addition, there can often be serious problems with poverty, even in cities in rich countries. Also some 'mega-cities' have become extremely large, and are still getting larger. In my country, Bangladesh, the capital Dhaka now has a population of about 17 million. The traffic is so bad that it has become almost impossible to move around the city during the day, and it seems certain that there are many children there who have never seen the countryside. This seems to me an unnatural way to live.

In conclusion, I think that the rapid increase in the size of cities is probably a negative thing. However, there are still reasons why people choose to move to them. It is likely that many cities will continue to increase for many years to come.

City transport (pages 55–56)

2a **a)** It shows the popularity of types of transport in one city in 2015. **b)** train **c)** taxi

2b **a)** subway **b)** motorbike, bicycle **c)** car, foot
d) taxi, subway, train

3a

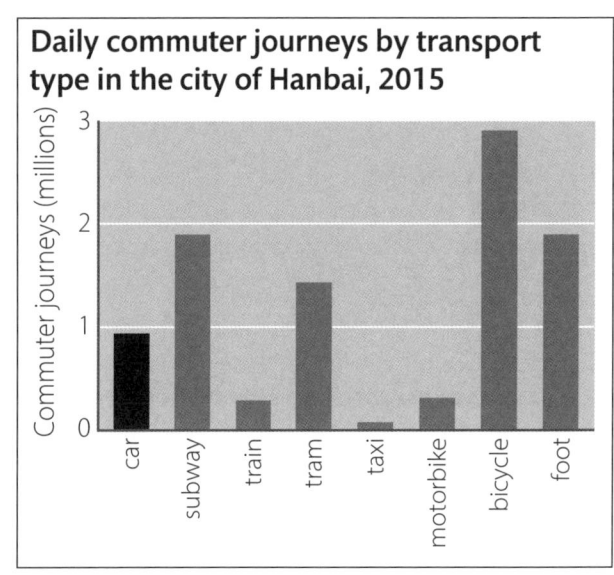

Daily commuter journeys by transport type in the city of Hanbai, 2015

3b

Giving approximate figures	Comparing figures
just over around nearly just under	three times that number five times that number two thirds as many

4   Sample answers

The chart shows the number of journeys taken each day by various forms of transport in a European city. The information is for the years 1985 and 2015.

In 1985, there were just under 60,000 journeys each day by bus, which made it the most popular form of transport. There were just a tenth of that number by train, which was the least popular form. Approximately 15,000 journeys each day were by subway, while just over double that number were by car. There were around 8,000 journeys by bicycle, while about three times that number of journeys were on foot.

Thirty years later, the figures for all forms of transport except train travel had changed. The bus was still the most popular form of travel, but the number of journeys was down to slightly more than 40,000 per day. Around half that number of journeys were on the subway. Around 35,000 journeys were made by car. Just under 20,000 journeys were by bicycle, but nearly twice as many were on foot.

Too many cars (pages 57–58)

2a   2 e **3** a **4** d **5** c **6** f

2b   2 can **3** will **6** may

3   Possible answers 2 has built / is building **3** have been **4** can be **5** may be **6** did not expect **7** can help **8** will want **9** can cause **10** may be **11** will end **12** will increase **13** are asking **14** will not happen

4   Sample answer

Around the world, air travel has increased in popularity in recent years. Planes are one of the causes of pollution which leads to global warming. In this essay I will discuss whether there should be a high tax on air travel.

20 years ago, people flew less often than they do now. Since then, many new airlines have started, and ticket prices have come down. Now it is normal for people in some countries to fly several times a year. If air travel keeps becoming more popular, it will cause more and more pollution. One way to get people to fly less it to put a high tax on plane tickets. However, this may not be the best way.

A high tax on plane tickets is not very fair. People want to have holidays abroad. Some people might need to fly for work or family reasons. A high tax on air travel could cause problems for millions of ordinary people. On the other hand, most rich people will probably not care about the extra cost. I think a better solution is for people to change their habits. For example, more people could have business meetings over the internet, instead of meeting face to face. Instead of flying for three short holidays every year, people could fly for one longer holiday instead.

In conclusion, I believe that it is a good idea to try and reduce the amount of air travel, or at least to stop it increasing. However, I do not think that a high tax on air travel is the answer. It is not a fair solution.

Improve your work! (pages 59–60)

1   The two pie charts show the average audience shares for the terrestrial channels of a European country in 1999 and 2009.

In 1999, there were six channels. Channel 1 had the largest proportion, at 40%. Next were Channels 2 and 3 with 14% and 25%. Sport TV had a share of 11%, while Art Media's share was just over half that figure. News Today had the smallest audience share at 4%.

Ten years later, there were three new channels. Films Plus had the largest audience share with 15%. Comedy Station, and Kids TV had 9% and 4%. The decline was not evenly spread among the other channels. News Today's share did not change, and Sport TV's share went down by just one percent. In contrast, Channels 1 to 3 all lost a large proportion of their audience. Channel 1's share dropped to 26%, Channel 2's to 10%, and Channel 3's to 19%. The biggest drop was Art media, which lost half its audience share.

2   1 governments give / the government gives
2 this is a good way
3 very small audiences / a very small audience
4 can hold **5** a few hundred people **6** are only seen
7 comes **8** who have worked hard **9** will never see
10 they have paid **11** better to spend **12** things

3

	yes	no
uses paragraphs		✓
repeats words or ideas too many times	✓	
uses the same words as the task question	✓	
always writes in an academic style		✓
sometimes uses complex sentences	✓	
uses linking words	✓	
always stays on the topic of the question		✓
makes clear arguments and answers the question well		✓
writes 250 words		✓

4   Sample answers

'On demand' TV services such as Netflix are becoming increasing popular. In this essay I will discuss whether I believe this is a positive or a negative development.

Most on demand TV is not free. To use it, you have to pay a small monthly fee. I cannot see any reason why I would pay to get something which I can get for free from regular broadcast TV. It seems just another way for companies to get more money from people. In my country there are already around 50 regular TV channels to choose from. That seems enough to me.

As far as I am aware, most on demand TV services are American. Many of these shows are excellent, but if everybody is watching American shows on the internet around the world, it will have a bad effect on national TV channels and national companies which make TV shows. I believe that national television is a valuable part of our culture, and it is important to keep it.

In my experience, people like to discuss popular TV shows the day after they are broadcast. It gives people a topic of conversation, and it helps to bring people together. If everybody has watched something different the evening before, then this opportunity will be lost.

In conclusion, I believe that the only benefit of 'on demand' TV is that it is convenient to start watching a show when you want to. In every other respect, I think its increase in popularity is a negative development.

Test Task 1 (page 61)

Band 4 score

Many people like to come to one town in The UK as tourists from other coutries In first chart there is information about the years 2011 and 2015. We can see information about three countries, India, Czech Republic and United Arab Emirates. in other chart we see how many visitors to UK. there many people from Czech coming to a town in the UK in 2015 and not many from United Arab Emirates. in India more people come to the UK in 2011. number of people coming from United Arab Emirates is going up and down between 2011 and 2015. more peple come to the UK in 2015 than 2011, number is going up every year, this is maybe becaus there are more adverts about the UK and more people want to visit UK as tourists

(136 words)

Examiner commentary

There is no introduction or overview sentence, so it is difficult for the reader to understand what the charts are about.

The answer is too short. It needs to be at least 150 words.

The writing isn't organised into paragraphs and there is a lack of punctuation. This makes it difficult to follow the argument.

In IELTS Writing Task 1, you don't need to give your opinion. You need to describe the data. The writer gives an opinion about

adverts for the UK. However, there is no information about adverts in the charts.

The writer does not use information from the bar charts. It is important to describe the charts, using data.

The language used is simple. Sentences are short and no complex structures are used.

There are many spelling errors and at some points these errors make the writing difficult to understand (e.g. ~~coutries~~ countries, ~~peple~~ people).

There are many grammar mistakes (~~In first chart~~, In the first chart).

There is no attempt to link information clearly across sentences. Each sentence describes something different. The writer doesn't build up a clear picture of what the graphs tell us.

Band 5.5 score

The charts shows visitor numbers to a town in the UK from 2011 to 2015. One chart show the number of tourists who visit this town from three countries (India, Czech Republic and United Arab Emirates. Other chart shows total oversees tourists to this town between 2011 and 2015.

The Number of tourists to this town in the UK went up from 1,100 in 2011 to 4,600 in 2015. Visitors from India went up from around 350 in 2011 to about 420 in 2015. Visitor numbers went down in 2012. Visitor numberss from UAE also went up, from 240 in 2011 to just under 350 in 2015. They went down in 2014. Visitor numbers from the Czech Republic also went up from around 275 in 2011 to over 450 in 2015. This was the bigest increase of all countries.

To sum up, the coutries in the chart follow similar patten to total number visitors to one town in the UK. This shows that visitor numbers have gone up.
(168 words)

Examiner commentary

The text has a clear introduction and the writer doesn't copy the same words from the question.

The writer uses paragraphs.

The information is clearly organised. The writer starts with an overview, explaining what the data is about. Then the writer describes the main features of the data, before finishing with a conclusion paragraph.

The writer clearly uses data from the graphs.

Although the meaning is generally clear, there are problems with noun verb agreement (~~The charts shows~~ The charts show), articles (~~Other chart shows~~ The other chart shows). The writer uses the same words and phrases too often (go down, go up, the number of tourists) and choice of vocabulary at times (fall down).

There are also some spelling mistakes, but these don't interfere with the message (~~bigest~~ biggest, ~~patten~~ pattern). There are also some punctuation errors (~~The Number of tourists~~ The number of tourists).

The writer uses a range of grammar structures to talk about the present and the past.

The conclusion focuses on comparing the trends on the two charts.

Test Task 2 (page 61)

Band 4 score

These days, many people rely on their mobile phones for example communicating with friends, getting news. It is a positive devlopment. for example first of all, people communicating with friends and take photos. peple use mobile phones for everything. peopl taking photos email and message their friends. My friends all have mobile phones. I find out where my friends are very easy. My friends have their mobile phones all time. It is also good for to answer many questions. If you want know the answer to question, you use the internet. You know the answer very qiuckly. You do not need remember things anymore. The same with peoples phone numbers. I don't need remeber anyone's number anymore. Another thing is the games and apps on my phone. Games and apps are entertainning. I always have something to do where I have my phone. Is good if you are on long very boring journey. You can watch TV on phones, too. So, in my opinion, there is so many positives about mobile phones and people need to have them because they make the life better and easier and also nowadays they are not very expensive you can have internet everywhere in the world.

(202 words)

Examiner commentary

The answer is short. It needs to be at least 250 words.

The answer isn't organised into paragraphs.

Sentences are mainly short and simple.

In the first paragraph, words are copied from the question.

There is a lack of referencing and substitution. The writer repeats words and phrases (e.g. people, friends) instead of using different words, or reference words such as *it* or *they*.

There is some attempt at linking with words and phrases like *first of all*, *Another thing* and *So*.

Some good points are made, but there is not much progression in the argument. It is more of a list of points. The writer probably hasn't planned the answer.

There is a conclusion, but it doesn't summarise the arguments in the essay. It adds new ideas.

The answer only focuses on positive things. The writer does not consider both sides of the argument.

There are many errors with spelling (~~devlopment~~ development) and punctuation (sometimes, it is difficult to understand where a sentence begins or ends).

There are many grammatical errors (~~people communicating with friends~~ people communicate with friends).

Band 5.5 score

Mobile phones getting more advanced recently. In past, people just using mobile phones to call people and they was very big. These days, they can do many more things. People can do their shopping, send text massage, take photos, email people and even run business from them. In this essay I will discuss if this a positive or a negative thing.

Many people think that mobile phones are positive. A mobile phone is a very small which you can carry it everywhere. You can write emails, call people and take photos any time. People have music on their phones to. They listen to them when they doing exercise. They can also watch movies, TV and read the news. These small gadgets do so much, so many people take them everywhere and rely on them for many different things.

But rely on your mobile phone too much can be negative. People fall in love with their mobile phones, which they use for everything. It means that they do not need their brains as much. All important information is on their mobile phone. So, this makes people lazy, which may not be good. And, if things go wrong with the phone, people have problems. So, for example, if battery run out, you may not able contact people. If you lose your phone, you may lose all you information, like photos and numbers.

I think mobile phones have many positive things. However, I think people need be careful with them. They should also keep a record of the information on their phone in case it is lost.

(264 words)

Examiner commentary

There is a clear introduction. The writer explains what the essay will focus on.
The writer uses paragraphing to separate the argument into intro, positives, negatives and conclusion.

The sentences are usually basic, but some complex sentences are attempted. Some of these are successful (People fall in love with their mobile phones, which they use for everything), and some of them are not (~~A mobile phone is a very small which you can carry it everywhere.~~ A mobile phone is a very small thing which you can carry everywhere.).
There are some grammar errors, usually when the candidate wants to say something complex (~~Mobile phones getting more advanced recently~~ Mobile phones have been getting more advanced recently). However, these errors do not usually make the meaning unclear.
To avoid repetition, more referencing could be used (e.g. using it instead of repeating the word mobile phone).
There is a good conclusion, giving the writer's opinion and summarising the arguments in the essay.

Mathematics for Learning a... ...t...ing

STAGE TWO
manual for MaLT tests

8 9 10 11

MANUAL

Standardised mathematics assessment
and error analysis for screening,
monitoring and teaching

HODDER
EDUCATION
AN HACHETTE UK COMPANY

The **Mathematics Assessment for Learning and Teaching (MaLT)** series was developed and standardised for the publishers by the University of Manchester.

Project Director: Professor Julian Williams
Project Coordinator: Lawrence Wo
Project Team: Constantia Hadjidemetriou, Iasonas Lamprianou, Sarah Lewis
Consultants: Brian Doig, Francis Eade, Gill Hunter, Avril Hutton, Carol Jones

Hachette UK's policy is to use papers that are natural, renewable and recyclable products and made from wood grown in sustainable forests.
The logging and manufacturing processes are expected to conform to the Environmental regulations of the country of origin.

Orders: please contact Bookpoint Ltd, 130 Milton Park, Abingdon, Oxon OX14 4SB. Telephone: (44) 01235 827720. Fax: (44) 01235 400454. Lines are open from 9.00 to 5.00, Monday to Saturday, with a 24-hour message answering service. You can also order through our website www.hodderheadline.co.uk.

British Library Cataloguing in Publication Data
A catalogue record for this title is available from the British Library

ISBN 978 1 444 10256 7

First published 2009
Impression number   11
Year   2015

Printed in Great Britain for Hodder Education, an Hachette UK Company, 338 Euston Road, London NW1 3BH, by Hobbs the Printers Ltd, Totton, Hampshire SO40 3WX.

Contents

MaLT – Mathematics Assessment for Learning and Teaching – offers a ground-breaking new approach to standardised, diagnostic assessment, which provides a *complete* Mathematics assessment package for ages 4:0–15:5.

Available in both pencil-and-paper *and* interactive computer-adaptive (CAT) formats, these nationally standardised tests – for groups or individuals – also yield diagnostic information which will directly support individual and whole-class teaching.

There is more information in children's responses than merely whether they are right or wrong. Teachers (and potentially children themselves) can use **diagnostic error analysis** to interpret particular responses and response patterns, and teachers can interpret particular patterns for their class and use these formatively to inform their teaching. **MaLT** assessments were *purpose-written* to highlight particular errors and misunderstandings which are diagnostic of key learning needs, such as counting errors, misconceptions with decimals, limited conceptions of shape, etc.

MaLT also provides the summative measures of performance needed for screening, monitoring and progress assessment. **MaLT** tests have been age-standardised nationally, ensuring secure, reliable norm-referenced standardised scores for pupils of different ages.

MaLT samples all aspects of mathematics from Reception to Year 9 in England & Wales, generating comprehensive assessments and providing:

- standardised scores, percentiles and National Curriculum levels, *plus*
- year-on-year *progress* assessment
- pupil 'performance maps'
- *individualised* formative and diagnostic feedback to pupils
- *whole-class* profiles identifying relative strengths and weaknesses, and common misconceptions and errors.

For every child, a personalised, diagnostic report – generated automatically by computer-adaptive assessment; or computer-aided (via the user-friendly **Scorer/Profiler CD-ROM**) from the paper-and-pencil tests – is available, directly informing individual or class teaching.

The series includes additionally a photocopiable book/CD pack providing six *standardised* **Diagnostic Mental Mathematics Tests**, a 'stand-alone' package covering National Curriculum levels 3–5.

This dual formative–summative design will help schools and teachers to maintain rigorous standardised assessment and recording of progress while also developing *formative* assessment – 'assessment for learning' – that informs teaching and learning. **MaLT** will also support schools in moving from paper-and-pencil group screening of whole classes to individually-adapted computer assessment, on an assessment-when-ready basis.

MaLT has been carefully matched to the strands and learning objectives of the Primary and Secondary Frameworks for Mathematics, and has been standardised nationally on over 12500 pupils. The distribution of questions by strand, attainment target and National Curriculum level within each test can be seen in the photocopiable *Class Record Sheets* provided at the end of this Manual.

Which test(s) should I use?

MaLT can be used at any time during the school year – for screening, monitoring and tracking progress, as well as for individual diagnostic profiling – and is available in both pencil-and-paper and computer-adaptive formats.

Pencil-and-paper assessment

Each pencil-and-paper test is designed to assess pupils across a wide range of ability within a specific year group, as indicated in Table 1. (Tests 5, 6 and 7 are administered orally by the teacher, to ensure that assessment of pupils' mathematical attainment is not masked by possible difficulties with *reading* questions.)

Table 1

Test	Norms for chronological ages (years:months)	Year group		
		England & Wales	Scotland	Northern Ireland
MaLT 5	4:0 to 6:5	Reception	Primary 1	Year 1
MaLT 6	5:0 to 7:5	Year 1	Primary 2	Year 2
MaLT 7	6:0 to 8:5	Year 2	Primary 3	Year 3
MaLT 8	7:0 to 9:5	Year 3	Primary 4	Year 4
MaLT 9	8:0 to 10:5	Year 4	Primary 5	Year 5
MaLT 10	9:0 to 11:5	Year 5	Primary 6	Year 6
MaLT 11	10:0 to 12:5	Year 6	Primary 7	Year 7
MaLT 12	11:0 to 13:5	Year 7	Secondary 1	Year 8
MaLT 13	12:0 to 14:5	Year 8	Secondary 2	Year 9
MaLT 14	13:0 to 15:5	Year 9	Secondary 3	Year 10

If your primary concern is to assess and monitor progress, pupils can be given the appropriate pencil-and-paper test every year, usually toward the *end* of the school year. The year-on-year coverage provided by the tests 5–14 will enable you to use **MaLT** as an indicator of progress made by your pupils throughout the school, and of 'value-added'.

The test may also be used in a diagnostic and formative manner, when it should preferably be used at the *beginning* of each school year to indicate strengths and weaknesses, to check to see if there has been any fall-back since the end of the previous year, and to provide information which will enable your lesson planning and target setting to be fully informed. The **Scorer/ Profiler** facilitates detailed diagnostic analysis and year-on-year progress monitoring, and generates individual and group performance reports.

Computer-adaptive on-screen assessment

Computer-adaptive assessment is sensitive to each pupil's answers on the test, selecting and presenting new questions that are optimally matched to the pupil's performance. As such, it provides individually differentiated assessment which is tailored to the attainment of the individual pupil. This technique enables **MaLT** to explore each pupil's mathematical knowledge, understanding and skills at the limits of his or her own ability, yielding a finely textured profile of what he or she can and cannot do. It also makes for highly efficient and effective assessment that significantly reduces teacher workload.

Fully computerised and networkable, the intuitive and fully interactive on-screen presentation gives instant analysis and results: National Curriculum levels and age-standardised scores (based on a minimum number of items per test) *plus* personalised feedback to support assessment for learning and focus support. Pupil reports and group performance analyses can highlight strengths and pinpoint specific weaknesses at both individual and whole-class levels.

MaLT computer-adaptive packages are available in Single-user and Network versions, and are suitable for use from about age 8 (i.e. when pupils can read the on-screen questions independently) to 14.

MaLT gives both summative and formative information:

- if you simply want to track the progress of your pupils from year to year, **MaLT** provides quick and convenient tests which are matched to the Frameworks for teaching mathematics and sample the full maths curriculum;

- if you need to establish a National Curriculum level for each pupil, **MaLT** tests are calibrated to indicate National Curriculum levels, subdivided into upper, middle and lower – a, b and c – to provide a finer level of information;

- if you need externally norm-referenced, age-standardised scores for value-added requirements, **MaLT** tests will provide them;

- if you wish to investigate the particular strengths and weaknesses of individual pupils or whole classes, and probe misconceptions and misunderstandings, **MaLT** tests and reporting software are designed specifically with this in mind.

Because it has a diagnostic, formative capability, **MaLT** enables you to answer such questions as:

- How has *this* child done compared to others of his/her age or year group?

- What is a reasonable level of achievement for pupils of this age in this year group?

- What are the strengths or successes of this pupil, or the class?

- What important, common errors are the pupils in my class making?

- On what aspects of the subject should the pupils concentrate to make sure they achieve the highest standard?

The information in this Teacher's Manual introduces you to a wealth of diagnostic information that can enable you to be more effective in the management of learning in your classroom.

The **MaLT** summative scores – standardised score, percentile, mathematics age, national curriculum level – will let you follow progress, measure value-added and provide a set of validated data for future years. The pattern revealed will in turn inform the target-setting process.

Equally, **MaLT** will highlight those mathematical skills in which pupils are confident and those that need addressing. The personalised 'performance map' provided by the Scorer/Profiler for each pupil (see page 47) pinpoints the tasks the pupil answered correctly, where the pupil went wrong, and the mistakes they made.

MaLT 8–11 each consist of 45 mark points and whilst pupils should be allowed enough time to attempt all of the questions, each test will take approximately 45 minutes.

Ensure that any support material around the classroom – such as number lines, multiplication tables or other mathematical posters – are taken down or covered up for the duration of these tests.

1   Each pupil will need a test booklet, a pen or pencil and – for **MaLT 11** only – a calculator. Rubbers may be used.

2   Instruct the pupils to fill in their details and read the instructions on the front cover.

3   Remind the pupils:

■   Try each question but if there is any one you cannot do, go on to the next one and come back to it later.

■   Show your working on the booklet itself.

■   If you make a mistake, cross (or rub) it out and write the correct answer clearly.

■   When you have finished, go back and check your answers.

■   For **MaLT 11**, pupils should stop at the end of the calculator section and wait until calculators have been collected in before moving onto the non-calculator section.

4   When everyone is ready, tell the pupils to open their booklets. Pupils should be given as long as necessary to complete the paper, but these tests will normally take about 45 minutes.

5   You should answer questions concerning the test procedure or unfamiliar contexts, but should not explain any mathematical terms.

Marking and recording results

Summative marking

To access *summative* test results – standardised score, percentile, National Curriculum level or maths age – it is necessary only to refer to the mark scheme on page 11, score each item right or wrong, award one mark for each correct response, and then total these marks to obtain an overall raw score. You can then go directly to the appropriate conversion table in this Manual to access the result(s) you require.

To be credited, pupils' responses must be clear and unambiguous, for example:

■   if the pupil ticked rather than circled an answer;

■   if the answer is numerically/algebraically equivalent (unless otherwise specified in the mark scheme).

If more than one answer is given, when only one is required, then award no mark even if one of the answers given is correct. Do not award half-marks.

Marking the same double-page spreads together rather than going through each test booklet as a whole is often quicker if you have many scripts to mark, as this gives you time to familiarise yourself with the mark scheme.

The front cover of the test booklet provides spaces to record the 'calculator score' and 'non-calculator score'. These are an aid to record-keeping and can *not* be used to compare calculator-mathematics and non-calculator-mathematics achievements.

Diagnostic marking

Diagnostic marking is recommended if you wish to get the maximum information from each pupil's performance on the test. You can do this for all pupils, or perhaps just for selected individuals.

To analyse individual performance by *strand*, refer to the mark scheme, where each question is categorised, as follows:

CN Counting and Understanding Number
NF Knowing and Using Number Facts
Ca Calculating
Sh Understanding Shape
Me Measuring
HD Handling Data

These codings are also shown on the photocopiable *Class Record Sheets*.

The **MaLT** tests were written with a view to 'revealing' errors that are diagnostic of some stage of development, common error or misconception. The standardisation of the tests highlighted the errors that could be considered significant, and each such significant error is coded in the mark scheme: some questions did not elicit a clear significant error-type, whereas others elicited up to four error-types (coded 3, 4, 5, 6 in the mark scheme). This coding is the basis for diagnostic error analysis and reporting.

In the printed test booklets, the error code or codes associated with each question are printed immediately to the right of that question's mark box in the right-hand margin, for example:

3
4

If the pupil's answer is correct, put a **1** in the mark box. If the pupil has answered incorrectly, check in the mark scheme whether this response corresponds to the error coded as **3** or **4**: if so, simply circle the appropriate number, otherwise record a **9** to represent any other (less clearly significant) incorrect response. Record **9** also if the pupil has not recorded a response but has done some working out – indicating at least some attempt at answering the question.

If a question has not been attempted at all – with no response or working out – put a **0** in the box.

For example, consider **MaLT 11**, question 7, involving finding the difference between two numbers, the coding is as follows:

Pupil's response	Marking code
110	**1** (*correct answer*)
120	**3** made 'counting by 5s' error in a perimeter task
45	**4** multiplied visible numbers and objects in perimeter task

To summarise:

The response codings are:	**1** for the correct answer
	3, 4, 5, 6 diagnostic error codings
	9 for any other incorrect response
	0 if no answer given: question omitted

Class record sheet

You can enter these codings into the photocopiable *Class Record Sheet* provided at the end of this Manual in order to see at a glance the performance of pupils on the test as a whole and to identify potentially significant *patterns* of performance on individual items by the class – helping you to pinpoint questions and topics that may need further work.

Using the Scorer/Profiler CD-ROM

Each pupil's set of codings, as above, can be keyed into the Scorer/Profiler, or entered first into an Excel spreadsheet and then imported electronically – useful if you are working with a full class.

It is also possible to mark each test booklet *directly* from/into the Scorer/Profiler software, without needing to hand-score it first. (This is a useful option if you have access to clerical assistance, as marking in this way does not require any specific mathematical knowledge or expertise.)

Whichever approach you prefer to input your own test data, the Scorer/Profiler will automatically calculate all the results for each pupil, and generate a range of analyses and summative reports as well as diagnostic feedback at both individual and group levels. Alternatively, if you do not require diagnostic information, you can simply input total raw scores in order to generate summative analyses and reports.

Full instructions are given in the User's Guide included on the Scorer/Profiler CD-ROM.

Obviously, the *computer-adaptive* versions of **MaLT** fully automate the whole process of diagnostic error analysis, as well as summative reporting.

MaLT 8 mark scheme

The objective descriptions for correct answers have been taken/adapted from the Primary Framework and National Curriculum level descriptors.

Question	Code	Response	Objective/Error Description
1a (CN)	✓	82, 102	**Recognise and continue number sequences formed by counting on or back in steps of constant size**
	error 3	82,*	can count-on in tens from a 2-digit number up to 100, but made error counting through 100
1b (CN)	✓	405, 105	**Recognise and continue number sequences formed by counting on or back in steps of constant size**
2 (CN)	✓	90	**Read, write and order whole numbers to at least 1000 and position them on a number line**
	error 3	82	made a counting error
	error 4	99	either made a counting error or misinterpreted 'nearest to' as 'appears like'
3a (NF)	✓	40	**Derive and recall all addition and subtraction facts for ... number pairs that total 100**
3b (NF)	✓	21	**Derive and recall all addition and subtraction facts for ... number pairs that total 100**
	error 3	31	made error in counting by tens to 100
	error 4	20 **or** 30	ignored units in counting-on problem
4a (CN)	✓	1 sector or equiv.	**Read and write proper fractions (e.g. 3/7, 9/10), interpreting the denominator as the parts of a whole and the numerator as the number of parts**
	error 3	4 sectors	ignored the fraction: 'one-quarter is 4'
4b (CN)	✓	2 sectors or equiv.	**Use diagrams to compare fractions and establish equivalents**
	error 3	1 sector	ignored the fractions denominator: shaded 1/8 for 1/4, suggesting a unit-fraction conception prototype
	error 4	4 sectors	ignored the fraction: 'one-quarter is 4'
5 (CN)	✓	100, 60	**Count on from and back to zero in single-digit steps or multiples of 10**
6 (CN)	✓	7301, 306	**Partition three-digit numbers into multiples of 100, 10 and 1 in different ways**
	error 3	only 1 correctly circled, with none or just one incorrectly circled	identifies some hundreds digits appropriately, but sometimes confuses units, tens, thousands with hundreds columns

* represents any number

Question	Code	Response	Objective/Error Description
7a (Ca)	✓	11	**Add or subtract mentally combinations of one-digit and two-digit numbers**
7b (Ca)	✓	13	**Add or subtract mentally combinations of one-digit and two-digit numbers**
	error 3	17	wrote 20 − 7 = 17, suggesting an avoidance of the count-down strategy
8 (Ca)	✓	1.8	**Refine and use efficient written methods to add and subtract two-digit and three-digit whole numbers and £-p**
	error 3	180	ignored decimal point in £p problem
	error 4	1.08 **or** 18p	made a place-value error in a money problem
9a (Me)	✓	6	**Read, to the nearest division and half-division, scales that are numbered or partially numbered**
	error 3	5	made estimation error in 'half-way between' problem
9b (Me)	✓	60	**Read, to the nearest division and half-division, scales that are numbered or partially numbered**
	error 3	55	counted intervals as prototypical 'ones' on a scale
	error 4	20	made comprehension error in a word problem, suggesting problem with concept: 'between'
10 (CN)	✓	A **and** D	**Identify and estimate fractions of shapes**
	error 3	incl. E	identified 1/5 as a quarter, suggesting a ratio misconception of the 'unit' base of the fraction
	error 4	only A **or** A with one wrong	partially understood 'one-quarter' but distracted by some features or 'unusual' cases, suggesting an early prototypical conception of fraction
11 (Me)	✓	from 165 upto but not including 175	**Read, choose, use and record standard metric units to estimate and measure length, weight and capacity to a suitable degree of accuracy (e.g. the nearest cm)**
	error 3	160 **or** 180	made a rounding error, suggesting that 'to the nearest 10' is understood as 'to within ten of'
12 (NF)	✓	30, 95, 5	**Recognise multiples of 2, 5 or 10 up to 1000**
	error 3	2 out of 3	identified only some of the multiples of 5
	error 4	51 included	identified 51 as a multiple of 5, suggesting confusion of numeral
13a (NF)	✓	48	**Use knowledge of number operations and corresponding inverses, including doubling and halving, to estimate and check calculations**
13b (NF)	✓	76	**Use knowledge of number operations and corresponding inverses, including doubling and halving, to estimate and check calculations**
	error 3	68	ignored the units digit when doubling a 2-digit number

Question	Code	Response	Objective/Error Description
14 (Ca)	✓	2	**Round remainders up or down, depending on the context**
	error 3	3	made a rounding error in a word problem
15 (Sh)	✓	D	**Describe, visualise, classify, draw and make the shapes**
	error 3	C	confused 'half turn' with 'quarter turn'
	error 4	B	confused 'half turn' with 'half a right-angle turn'
	error 5	A	confused 'half turn' and reflection
16 (Me)	✓	10:10	**Calculate time intervals and find start or end times for a given time interval**
	error 3	9:70	treated hours and minutes separately in a counting-on problem
17a (HD)	✓	15	**Answer a question by collecting, organising and interpreting data**
	error 3	3	ignored the key when interpreting charts
17b (HD)	✓	20	**Answer a question by collecting, organising and interpreting data**
	error 3	4	ignored the key when interpreting charts
	error 4	5	misunderstood word problem, suggesting misconception of 'more'
17c (HD)	✓	Maria, Nick	**Answer a question by collecting, organising and interpreting data**
18 (CN)	✓	930, 780	**Count on from and back to zero in single-digit steps or multiples of 10**
	error 3	*, 800	miscounted down by 30 through the 'hundreds' in a sequence suggesting prototype 'by tens'
	error 4	*, 790	miscounted down by 30 through the 'hundreds'
19 (CN)	✓	A, C, E	**Use diagrams to identify equivalent fractions (e.g. 6/8 and 3/4, or 70/100 and 7/10)**
	error 3	1 or 2 correct (with no incorrect answers)	has partial understanding of 1/2, but did not recognise 1/2 = 2/4 = 4/8, suggesting inflexibility with equivalence of simple fractions
	error 4	B included	wrote 4/4 for 4/8 shaded, suggesting a 'ratio' misconception
	error 5	D included	wrote 1/4 for 4/8, suggesting a unit-fraction misconception/prototype
20 (Ca)	✓	10	**Represent repeated addition and arrays as multiplication**
	error 3	36	probably misunderstood the question

* represents any number

Question	Code	Response	Objective/Error Description
21a (NF)	✓	YN	**Use knowledge of number operations and corresponding inverses**
	error 3	YY	appeared to believe that both addition and subtraction are commutative
21b (NF)	✓	YN	**Use knowledge of number operations and corresponding inverses**
	error 3	YY	appeared to believe that both multiplication and division are commutative
22 (Ca)	✓	19	**Develop and use written methods to record, support or explain addition and subtraction of two-digit and three-digit numbers**
	error 3	21	took smaller digits from larger digit in a subtraction calculation
	error 4	29	wrote 37 − 18 = 29, suggesting a 'bug' with carrying
	error 5	55	performed an addition instead of subtraction
23 (Me)	✓	14	**Read, to the nearest division and half-division, scales that are numbered or partially numbered**
	error 3	18	counted each interval of a scale as one unit, suggesting a unit-prototype
	error 4	15	misread a scale, suggesting either 'estimation' or a 'miswriting' error
24 (Me)	✓	2 litres	**Choose and use appropriate units to estimate, measure and record measurements**
25 (Sh)	✓	E	**Draw and complete shapes with reflective symmetry**
26 (Ca)	✓	167	**Develop and use written methods to record, support or explain addition and subtraction of two-digit and three-digit numbers**
27 (Ca)	✓	6	**Find unit fractions of numbers and quantities (e.g. 1/2, 1/3, 1/4 and 1/6 of 12 litres)**
	error 3	3	wrote '3' for '1/3'
	error 4	9	counted 1/2 a set instead of 1/3 of the set
28 (CN)	✓	812	**Partition three-digit numbers into multiples of 100, 10 and 1 in different ways**
	error 3	8012	wrote 8012 for 802, suggesting place-value misconception
	error 4	80012	wrote 80012 for 802, suggesting place-value misconception

Question	Code	Response	Objective/Error Description
29 (Ca)	✓	$60 \div 12$	**Develop and use written methods to record, support and explain multiplication and division of two-digit numbers by a one-digit number**
	error 3	$12 \div 60$	apparently 'partially recognised a multiplicative situation' by representing $60 \div 12$ as $12 \div 60$
	error 4	12×60	apparently 'partially recognised a multiplicative situation' by representing $60 \div 12$ as 12×6
30 (Me)	✓	2:45	**Read the time on a 12-hour digital clock and to the nearest 5 minutes on an analogue clock**
	error 3	3:45	confused hour of the clock with the next hour when reading a clock
	error 4	9:15	confused hour hand and minute hand on reading a clock
	error 5	2:15	read *quarter to* as *quarter past* on reading a clock
31 (NF)	✓	4×5, 2×10	**Derive and recall multiplication facts for the 2, 3, 4, 5, 6 and 10 times-tables and the corresponding division facts**
	error 3	pairs with one common number	selected calculations containing the same digits as having the same answers: 'the same is the same'
32a (Sh)	✓	A, D, F and G	**Describe, visualise, classify, draw and make the shapes**
	error 3	including C	identified a diamond as a triangle suggesting a 'triangle' misconception
32b (Sh)	✓	B, H, F and G	**Use a set-square to draw right angles and to identify right angles in 2-D shapes**
	error 3	B, C, E and H	identified only the rectangle as having 'right angles' suggesting 'right angle implies rectangle' misconception
	error 4	2 or 3 correct with none incorrect	recognised some but not all right-angled shapes
33a (CN)	✓	103	**Read, write and order whole numbers to at least 1000**
33b (CN)	✓	2014	**Read, write and order whole numbers to at least 1000**
	error 3	214 **or** 20014	misplaced digits in writing down number over 1000, suggesting place-value misconception
34 (Ca)	✓	any 2 correct numbers	**Understand that division is the inverse of multiplication and vice versa**
	error 3	division wrong way round (e.g. 1, 5)	wrote division in wrong order, suggesting the order of division is not yet understood
	error 4	pairs *adding* to 5 (e.g. 1, 4)	confused ÷ and + symbols

The objective descriptions for correct answers have been taken/adapted from the Primary Framework and National Curriculum level descriptors.

Question	Code	Response	Objective/Error Description
1 (CN)	✓	13	**Recognise and continue number sequences formed by counting on or back in steps of constant size**
2 (HD)	✓	9:15 (accept unambiguous ticks/ markings)	**Answer a question by identifying what data to collect**
	error 3	8:15	misinterpreted 'smallest number' in context as 'earliest time'
3 (NF)	✓	19	**Use knowledge of addition and subtraction facts and place value to derive sums and differences of pairs of multiples of 10, 100 or 1000**
	error 3	61	added instead of subtracted in 2-digit subtraction
	error 4	29	made a 'carry' error in 2-digit subtraction
	error 5	21	performed 'smaller from larger' error in a 2-digit horizontal subtraction
4a (Me)	✓	3	**Calculate time intervals from clocks and timetables**
4b (Me)	✓	8	**Calculate time intervals from clocks and timetables**
5 (Sh)	✓	C, F	**Compare angles with a right angle**
	error 3	F only	recognised some but not all right-angled triangles, suggesting a limited prototype conception of right-angled triangles
	error 4	incl. A	identified a trapezium as 'right angled' suggesting 'right angle' may be confused with 'rectangle'
6 (CN)	✓	51, 47	**Partition, round and order four-digit whole numbers**
	error 3	51 **or** 47only	rounded some but not all numbers 'to the nearest ten' correctly
	error 4	59 incl.	rounded 'down' instead of 'to the nearest', suggesting a reluctance to round-up the tens digit
7a (HD)	✓	43 in LHS	**Use Venn diagrams or Carroll diagrams to sort data and objects using more than one criterion**
	error 3	43 in middle	incorrectly placed number in the intersection set on a Venn diagram, suggesting partial understanding of Venn representation

Question	Code	Response	Objective/Error Description
7b (HD)	✓	40 in middle	**Use Venn diagrams or Carroll diagrams to sort data and objects using more than one criterion**
	error 3	40 in LHS **or** RHS	incorrectly placed number that should have been placed in the intersection set on a Venn diagram, suggesting partial understanding of Venn representation
8 (CN)	✓	3.05	**Use decimal notation for tenths and hundredths and partition decimals; relate the notation to money**
	error 3	3.5(0)	wrote £3.5(0) for £3.05, suggesting a place-value misconception
	error 4	305	missed a decimal point in writing down £ and p
	error 5	8 **or** 0.8	ignored coin values when counting up money
9 (Me)	✓	5900	**Interpret intervals and divisions on partially numbered scales and record readings accurately**
	error 3	5009	misread the intervals on a scale as units and counted up in ones, suggesting a prototype misconception of scales
	error 4	5090	misread the intervals on a scale as *tens* and counted back in tens, suggesting a prototype misconception of scales
	error 5	5999	misread the intervals on a scale as *units* and counted back in ones, suggesting a prototype misconception of scales
10 (Me)	✓	18	**Measure and calculate the perimeter of regular and irregular polygons**
	error 3	17 **or** 22	found perimeter by counting squares (instead of lengths/edges) surrounding a shape
	error 4	14	found perimeter by counting squares (instead of lengths/edges) on the inside of a shape
11 (Me)	✓	10(th)	**Use a calendar to calculate time intervals**
	error 3	3(rd)	missed one condition of a three-part word problem
	error 4	12 **or** 26(th)	missed two conditions of a three-part word problem
12 (HD)	✓	7	**Answer a question by identifying what data to collect**
	error 3	6	misread 'less than 11' as 'less than 10'
	error 4	9	misread 'less than 11' as '11 or less'
	error 5	2	misread 'less than 11' as 'equal to 11'
13 (Sh)	✓	B **and** D	**Draw polygons and classify them by identifying their properties, including their line symmetry**
	error 3	B only	identified the regular but not irregular hexagon, suggesting a prototype misconception
	error 4	A **and** E	confused *pentagon* with *hexagon*
	error 5	B **and** E	identified regular polygons as 'hexagons', suggesting a belief that only regular shapes have such names
	error 6	incl. F	identified six-pointed star as a hexagon, suggesting a vertex-misconception

Question	Code	Response	Objective/Error Description
14a (NF)	✓	6	**Derive and recall multiplication facts up to 10 × 10**
14b (NF)	✓	81	**Derive and recall multiplication facts up to 10 × 10, the corresponding division facts and multiples of numbers to 10 up to the tenth multiple**
	error 3	1	wrote 1 ÷ 9 = 9, suggesting a basic misunderstanding
	error 4	0	misread ÷ as an addition instruction
15 (HD)	✓	50	**Interpret the data in ... pictograms**
	error 3	5	ignored the key in a pictogram, suggesting a misconception of representation, 'one sign' is 'one object'
16 (CN)	✓	−10, −1, 0, 5, 20	**Use positive and negative numbers in context and position them on a number line**
	error 3	0, 1, 5, 10, 20	ignored the minus signs and ordered the integers by their magnitudes
	error 4	0, −10, −1, 5, 20	ordered integers with zero smallest, suggesting 'zero is the smallest number'
	error 5	−1, −10, 0, 5, 20	ordered integers partially correct: −ve then 0 then +ve, but placed −1 before −10, suggesting that integers are conceived of as two separate objects, 'the sign' and 'the number'
17a (Sh)	✓	C	**Draw the position of a shape after ... translation**
17b (Sh)	✓	2nd row, 3rd col.	**Know that angles are measured in degrees and that one whole turn is 360°**
18 (CN)	✓	3	**Use diagrams to identify equivalent fractions (e.g. 6/8 and 3/4, or 70/100 and 7/10)**
	error 3	4 or 7	missed one condition in a two-condition fractions problem
19 (CN)	✓	62.32	**Position one-place and two-place decimals on a number line**
	error 3	62.50	wrote 62.5(0) is less than 62.32, suggesting decimal point ignored
	error 4	68.10	ignored word-problem context and ordered numbers regardless
	error 5	65.13	ignored information in a table, suggesting the context was distracting
20 (CN)	✓	4570	**Explain what each digit represents in whole numbers**
	error 3	2570	misinterpreted a missing subtraction problem, suggesting unfamiliarity with format
21 (Me)	✓	2.4 correctly shown	**Interpret intervals and divisions on partially numbered scales and record readings accurately, where appropriate to the nearest tenth of a unit**
	error 3	2.2	misread intervals on a scale, suggesting a unit-interval prototype misconception
22 (Me)	✓	6	**Find the area of ... shapes drawn on a square grid by counting squares**
	error 3	10	attempted to calculate perimeter instead of area of a shape
	error 4	7	counted half-squares as whole squares when finding a shape's area
	error 5	5	counted whole squares only when finding a shape's area

Question	Code	Response	Objective/Error Description
23 (Ca)	✓	24 ÷ 4	**Support and explain multiplication and division of two-digit numbers by a one-digit number**
	error 3	24 × 4	selected × sign to model a ÷ problem, suggesting incomplete multiplicative conceptions
	error 4	4 ÷ 24	wrote ÷ sign in wrong order
24a (HD)	✓	6	**Answer a question by identifying what data to collect**
	error 3	**9 or 15**	misread a word problem, ignoring the 'more than' condition
24b (HD)	✓	8	**Answer a question by identifying what data to collect**
	error 3	22	ignored one condition in solving a two-condition word problem
25 (CN)	✓	10	**Use decimal notation for tenths and hundredths and partition decimals; relate the notation to money**
	error 3	200	wrote that there are 200 20p coins in £2
26 (Ca)	✓	296	**Refine and use efficient written methods to add and subtract two-digit and three-digit whole numbers**
	error 3	316	made a smaller-from-larger error in a 3-digit vertical subtraction
	error 4	306	made a carry-error in a 3-digit vertical subtraction, suggesting a place-value misconception
27 (CN)	✓	A, D and E	**Use diagrams to identify equivalent fractions (e.g. 6/8 and 3/4, or 70/100 and 7/10)**
	error 3	any other answer with C incl.	identified a fraction from unequal parts, suggesting a misconception/prototype for counting fractions
28 (NF)	✓	27 × 10 or 10 × 27	**Represent repeated addition and arrays as multiplication**
	error 3	other correct multiplication (e.g. 270 × 1)	identified a correct multiplication fact, but not the requested representation, 27 × 10
29 (NF)	✓	4	**Derive and recall multiplication facts up to 10 × 10, the corresponding division facts and multiples of numbers to 10 up to the tenth multiple**
	error 3	45	interpreted 'multiply' as 'add'
	error 4	3	answered suggesting 9 × 3 = 36, instead of 4
30 (Ca)	✓	3990	**Use efficient written methods to add and subtract whole numbers**
	error 3	3090, 3000 or 3900	wrote ten less than 4000 is 3090, 3000 or 3900, suggesting a place-value misconception and/or carrying error
31 (Sh)	✓	D and F	**Draw polygons and classify them by identifying their properties, including their line symmetry**
	error 3	D, G or F, G	identified some but not all asymmetrical shapes suggesting incomplete understanding of lines of symmetry

Question	Code	Response	Objective/Error Description
32 (Me)	✓	D	**Know the meaning of 'kilo', 'centi' and 'milli' and, where appropriate, use decimal notation to record measurements (e.g. 1.3 m or 0.6 kg)**
	error 3	C	wrote 2kg = 200g, suggesting 100g in a kg
	error 4	B	wrote 2kg = 20g, suggesting 10g in a kg
33a (CN)	✓	1100	**Recognise and continue number sequences formed by counting on or back in steps of constant size**
	error 3	1050, 1090, 1110 or 1150	counted up or down in 20s
	error 4	1140	counted up in 10s
33b (CN)	✓	980	**Recognise and continue number sequences formed by counting on or back in steps of constant size**
	error 3	1000 or 1020	counted up instead of down
	error 4	9080 or 9980	counted down with carrying error
	error 5	970	counted down by 40 instead of 30
34 (CN)	✓	4/6	**Find equivalent fractions (e.g. 7/10 = 14/20, or 19/10 = 1⁹⁄₁₀)**
	error 3	3/2	wrote 2/3 = 3/2, suggesting 'same difference, same value' additive misconception
	error 4	3/4 or 1/2	wrote 2/3 = 3/4 or 2/3 = 1/2, suggesting an 'additive' misconception
35 (NF)	✓	225	**Derive and recall multiplication facts up to 10 × 10, the corresponding division facts and multiples of numbers to 10 up to the tenth multiple**
	error 3	8 or 9	interpreted ÷ as × in a missing-value problem
36 (Me)	✓	E	**Choose and use standard metric units and their abbreviations when estimating, measuring and recording length, weight and capacity**
37 (Sh)	✓	D	**Draw the position of a shape after a reflection or translation**
	error 3	A	confused rotation with reflection
	error 4	B	confused translation and reflection
38a (Sh)	✓	(3,2)	**Read and plot coordinates in the first quadrant**
	error 3	(2,3)	reversed coordinates (x,y) with (y,x)
38b (Sh)	✓	(0,4)	**Read and plot coordinates in the first quadrant**
	error 3	(4,0)	reversed coordinates
	error 4	(1,4)	wrote (1,4) for (0,4), rejecting the zero coordinate
	error 5	(4,1)	wrote (4,1) for (0,4), rejecting the zero coordinate *and* reversing coordinates

The objective descriptions for correct answers have been taken/adapted from the Primary Framework and National Curriculum level descriptors.

Question	Code	Response	Objective/Error Description
1a (Ca)	✓	14	**Use efficient written methods to add and subtract whole numbers and decimals with up to two places**
	error 3	26	subtracted smaller from larger in a horizontal 2-digit subtraction
1b (Ca)	✓	20	**Calculate mentally with integers**
2 (Me)	✓	19	**Interpret intervals and divisions on partially numbered scales and record readings accurately**
	error 3	18 **or** 20	counted intervals as units in reading a scale
3a (CN)	✓	2	**Find equivalent fractions (e.g. 7/10 = 14/20)**
	error 3	1	made additive error when cancelling fractions
	error 4	8	doubled instead of halved when cancelling fractions
3b (CN)	✓	5	**Find equivalent fractions (e.g. 7/10 = 14/20)**
	error 3	2	wrote 1/2 = 5/25, suggesting a belief that $1 \times 1 = 2$
	error 4	10	wrote 1/10 = 2/25, suggesting a belief that $5 \times 10 = 25$
	error 5	21	made additive error when cancelling fractions
4 (Me)	✓	90	**Calculate time intervals from clocks and timetables**
	error 3	130, 1.3 or similar, **or** 150, 1.5 or similar	partially correctly calculated times from clocks, but incorrectly wrote down/converted between hours and minutes
5a (Ca)	✓	32	**Find fractions using division (e.g. 1/100 of 5 kg), and percentages of numbers and quantities (e.g. 10%, 5% and 15% of £80)**
	error 3	8	calculated 50% correctly, but misread the missing-value sentence in the problem
5b (Ca)	✓	64	**Find fractions using division (e.g. 1/100 of 5 kg), and percentages of numbers and quantities (e.g. 10%, 5% and 15% of £80)**
	error 3	4	calculated 'a quarter of' correctly, but misread the missing-value sentence in the problem
6a (Me)	✓	2200	**Convert larger to smaller units using decimals to one place (e.g. change 2.6 kg to 2600 g)**
	error 3	220	multiplied by 100 when converting kg to g

Question	Code	Response	Objective/Error Description
6b (Me)	✓	0.065	**Convert larger to smaller units using decimals to one place (e.g. change 2.6 kg to 2600 g)**
	error 3	0.65	divided by 100 when converting g to kg
	error 4	6.5	divided by 10 when converting g to kg
7 (Me)	✓	54	**Measure and calculate the perimeter of regular and irregular polygons**
	error 3	42	found perimeter = 7×6 instead of 9×6, suggesting either two sides missed or a multiplication-fact error
	error 4	90 or 126	included lengths of interior parts when calculating perimeter of a shape
8a (Ca)	✓	1621	**Use efficient written methods to add and subtract whole numbers and decimals with up to two places**
	error 3	1511 or 1521	made carrying error in addition problem
8b (Ca)	✓	468	**Refine and use efficient written methods to add and subtract two-digit and three-digit whole numbers**
	error 3	606	added instead of subtracted in a horizontal multi-digit subtraction
9 (CN)	✓	4 sections (or equiv.) shaded	**Find equivalent fractions (e.g. 7/10 = 14/20)**
	error 3	2 shaded	misunderstood 2/3 of as 2 parts of, suggesting lack of 'equivalent fractions' conception
	error 4	3 shaded	shaded 3/6 instead of 2/3
10a (CN)	✓	8	**Solve problems involving proportions of quantities**
	error 3	14	made additive error in missing-value proportion task
	error 4	80	ignored part of information in missing-value proportion task
10b (CN)	✓	15	**Solve problems involving proportions of quantities**
	error 3	12	made additive error in missing-value proportion task
11 (HD)	✓	3	**Answer a set of related questions by collecting, selecting and organising relevant data**
	error 3	1	ignored key in pictogram
	error 4	1.5	ignored key in pictogram and rounded down incorrectly
	error 5	10	ignored the 'more' in a 'how many' question
12 (Sh)	✓	B, C	**Use knowledge of properties to draw 2-D shapes, and to identify and draw nets of 3-D shapes**
	error 3	A, B	was partially correct in 3D-net task, but incorrectly included net of shape with lid
	error 4	B, E or C, E	was partially correct in 3D-net task, but included net with correct faces in wrong position

Question	Code	Response	Objective/Error Description
13 (HD)	✓	16	**Answer a set of related questions by collecting, selecting and organising relevant data**
	error 3	8	misinterpreted the intervals in a table
14 (Ca)	✓	2	**Use efficient written methods to add and subtract whole numbers and decimals with up to two places**
	error 3	3	rounded incorrectly during a division task
15 (Me)	✓	−15	**Interpret a reading that lies between two unnumbered divisions on a scale**
	error 3	+15	ignored the minus sign in a temperature reading
	error 4	−5	counted in wrong direction along a negative temperature scale
16a (HD)	✓	2	**Answer a set of related questions by collecting, selecting and organising relevant data**
	error 3	3	misinterpreted intervals in a table
	error 4	between 2 and 3	inappropriately interpolated an answer in a discrete-value context
16b (HD)	✓	9.50	**Answer a set of related questions by collecting, selecting and organising relevant data**
	error 3	6.60	misinterpreted intervals in a table
	error 4	any value between 6.60 and 9.50	inappropriately interpolated an answer in a discrete-value context
17a (CN)	✓	47, 62.5, 143	**Explain what each digit represents in whole numbers and decimals with up to two places, and partition, round and order these numbers**
	error 3	47, 143, 62.5	ignored the decimal point in an 'ordering' task
17b (CN)	✓	47, 62.36, 62.5, 62.72, 143	**Explain what each digit represents in whole numbers and decimals with up to two places, and partition, round and order these numbers**
	error 3	47, 62.5, 62.36, 62.72,143	ordered the whole numbers correctly, but places .5 before .36, suggesting the decimal is a 'pair of wholes'
	error 4	47, 143, 62.5, 62.36, 62.72	mis-ordered whole numbers before the decimals in an ordering problem
18 (Me)	✓	2.4 or equiv.	**Interpret a reading that lies between two unnumbered divisions on a scale**
	error 3	2.2	misreads interval prototypically as '1' on weighing scales
	error 4	2.5, 2½ or equiv. or 2¼	reads scales to nearest 1/2 or 1/4, ignoring decimals

Question	Code	Response	Objective/Error Description
19 (Ca)	✓	3.5	**Extend mental-methods for whole-number calculations**
	error 3	4	rounded up to a whole number in a travel time problem, suggesting a resistance to allow decimal numbers of hours
	error 4	3	rounded down to a whole number in a travel time problem, suggesting a resistance to allow decimal numbers of hours
20 (HD)	✓	45 in LHS, 56 in RHS	**Use Venn diagrams or Carroll diagrams to sort data and objects using more than one criterion**
	error 3	only one correct	was only partially correct in Venn diagram task
21 (Sh)	✓	B	**Know that angles are measured in degrees and that one whole turn is 360°**
	error 3	E	misinterpreted 90° as a half-turn
	error 4	A	confused anticlockwise with clockwise
22a (CN)	✓	3000	**Explain what each digit represents in whole numbers and ... round ... these numbers**
	error 3	4000	rounded up from 3458 to 4000, suggesting incorrect use of rules without understanding
	error 4	3500	misinterpreted 'to the nearest 1000' as 'to the nearest 100'
22b (CN)	✓	10000	**Explain what each digit represents in whole numbers and ... round ... these numbers**
	error 3	9000	rounded down instead of up from 9965, suggesting difficulty perceiving thousands as a 'unit'
	error 4	1000	wrote 1000 instead of 10000, suggesting place-value misconception
23 (CN)	✓	1(.0)	**Count from any given number in whole-number and decimal steps**
	error 3	0.10	counted 0.8, 0.9, 0.10, suggesting decimals as pairs of whole numbers separated by a point
	error 4	10	ignored the decimal, reading 0.8 as 8
	error 5	0.9	counted up by 1s, ignoring the size of the difference in a sequence
24a (Ca)	✓	8	**Use efficient written methods to add and subtract whole numbers**
	error 3	9	made a carrying error
	error 4	0, 1 **or** 5	attempted to subtract instead of adding in a 3-digit vertical addition
24b (Ca)	✓	3	**Extend mental-methods for whole-number calculations, for example to multiply a two-digit by a one-digit number (e.g. 12 × 9)**
	error 3	1	incorrectly multiplied by 7, suggesting a belief that $1 \times 7 = 1$

Question	Code	Response	Objective/Error Description
25 (Sh)	✓	(8, 3)	**Read and plot coordinates in the first quadrant**
	error 3	(3, 8)	wrote *x,y* coordinates in the wrong order
	error 4	(8, 2)	used partially correct coordinates, but miscounted in a sequence
26 (Sh)	✓	E	**Compare angles with a right angle**
	error 3	A	may have misperceived an angle as right-angled
	error 4	B	may have misconceived/interpreted 'right-angle' as 'rectangle'
27 (Sh)	✓	135	**Know that angles are measured in degrees and that one whole turn is 360°**
	error 3	45	calculated one part correctly in a two-part problem for a pie chart
28a (NF)	✓	4	**Derive and recall multiplication facts up to 10 × 10, the corresponding division facts and multiples of numbers to 10 up to the tenth multiple**
28b (NF)	✓	25	**Derive and recall multiplication facts up to 10 × 10, the corresponding division facts and multiples of numbers to 10 up to the tenth multiple**
	error 3	1	wrote $1 \div 5 = 5$, suggesting $\div$ is understood as 'divides into'
	error 4	0	wrote $0 \div 5 = 5$, suggesting $\div$ is read as 'difference'
	error 5	5	wrote $5 \div 5 = 5$
29 (CN)	✓	TFF	**State inequalities using the symbols < and > (e.g. –3 > –5, –1 < plus1)**
	error 3	TFT	ordered negatives as less than positives, but wrote $-5 > -1$, suggesting that the sign and the number are conceived as separate objects to be manipulated
	error 4	TTT	ignored minus signs of integers, e.g. $-10 > +7$ becomes $10 > 7$
30a (Ca)	✓1	1.21	**Use efficient written methods to add and subtract whole numbers and decimals with up to two places**
	error 3	0.58	wrote $0.7 + 0.51 = 0.58$, suggesting decimals are conceived as a pair of whole numbers separated by a point
30b (Ca)	✓	5.73	**Use efficient written methods to add and subtract whole numbers and decimals with up to two places**
	error 3	5.1(0) **or** 6(.0)	wrote $4.03 + 1.7 = 5.1(0)$, suggesting decimals are conceived as a pair of whole numbers separated by a point
	error 4	4.2(0)	wrote $4.03 + 1.7 = 4.20$, suggesting decimal point ignored

Question	Code	Response	Objective/Error Description
31 (Sh)	✓	D	**Draw the position of a shape after a reflection or translation**
	error 3	A	reflected shape in a vertical line, suggesting this may be a prototype
	error 4	B	translated a shape instead of reflecting in a sloping mirror
	error 5	C **or** E	correctly reflected in a sloping mirror, but positioned the image askew
32a (HD)	✓	2.5	**Construct and interpret ... line graphs**
	error 3	2 **or** 3	rounded times to nearest hour, suggesting a resistance to decimal numbers of hours
32b (HD)	✓	75	**Construct and interpret ... line graphs**
	error 3	150	misunderstood the time-distance graph
	error 4	30 **or** 90	misread scale on a time-distance grap

MaLT 11 mark scheme

The objective descriptions for correct answers have been taken/adapted from the Primary Framework and National Curriculum level descriptors.

Question	Code	Response	Objective/Error Description
1 (NF)	✓	175	**Derive and recall multiplication facts up to 10 × 10, the corresponding division facts and multiples of numbers to 10 up to the tenth multiple**
	error 3	7	divided instead of multiplied in missing-value problem
2 (Ca)	✓	8	**Use a calculator to solve problems, including those involving decimals**
3a (Ca)	✓	A and D	**Use a calculator to solve problems involving multi-step calculations**
	error 3	BD or ABD	was partially correct, but included an incorrect calculator sequence, suggesting a belief that subtraction is commutative
	error 4	A	was partially correct, but avoided multiplicative efficient method
	error 5	ACD	was partially correct, but included an incorrect calculator sequence, suggesting a belief that a calculator distributes subtraction over addition
3b (Ca)	✓	D	**Use a calculator to solve problems involving multi-step calculations**
	error 3	B	was partially correct, but included an incorrect calculator sequence, suggesting in a belief that subtraction is commutative
	error 4	A	was partially correct, but avoided multiplicative efficient method
4 (Ca)	✓	342	**Use a calculator to solve problems, including those involving decimals**
5a (CN)	✓	1.75	**Solve simple problems involving direct proportion by scaling quantities up or down**
5b (CN)	✓	500	**Solve simple problems involving direct proportion by scaling quantities up or down**
	error 3	5	completed one step in a two-step proportion task
5c (CN)	✓	0.84	**Solve simple problems involving direct proportion by scaling quantities up or down**
	error 3	1.05	incorrectly estimated a proportion in missing-value ratio task
	error 4	90	made an additive error in missing-value ratio task

Question	Code	Response	Objective/Error Description
6 (Ca)	✓	7044	**Use a calculator to carry out one-step and two-step calculations involving all four operations**
	error 3	70.44	incorrectly inserted a decimal point when reading money from a calculator display
	error 4	notational error with £,p	made a £ p notational error
7 (Sh)	✓	110	**Identify, visualise and describe properties of ... regular polygons; calculate the perimeter**
	error 3	120	made 'counting by 5s' error in a perimeter task
	error 4	45	multiplied visible numbers and objects in perimeter task
8a (HD)	✓	115	**Solve problems by ... interpreting data**
	error 3	118 **or** 138	read wrong row of a table
8b (HD)	✓	Wednesday	**Solve problems by ... interpreting data**
	error 3	Monday	misunderstood question, interpreting highest item as highest column total
9 (Ca)	✓	14	**Use a calculator to solve problems involving multi-step calculations**
	error 3	13	rounded down inappropriately in a division word problem
	error 4	15	may have rounded up twice to nearest whole in a division word problem
10 (Me)	✓	36	**Calculate the perimeter and area of rectilinear shapes**
	error 3	24	confused area and perimeter, and/or added only visible numbers on the figure
	error 4	28	confused area and perimeter
	error 5	40 **or** 52	calculated area of rectangle(s) not of whole compound shape
11a (HD)	✓	15.96	**Describe and interpret results and solutions to problems using the mode, range, median and mean**
	error 3	16	was partially correct, but rounded average to the nearest whole number of seconds
	error 4	16.23	confused mean and median averages
	error 5	15.37	confused mean and median averages and did not order the data
11b (HD)	✓	2.26	**Describe and interpret results and solutions to problems using the mode, range, median and mean**
	error 3	1.79	found range as difference between first and last of unordered set of data
12a (HD)	✓	12	**Solve problems by ... interpreting data**

Question	Code	Response	Objective/Error Description
12b (Me)	✓	4:05pm	**Calculate time intervals from clocks and timetables**
	error 3	3:65pm	writes 3:65pm for 4:05pm, treating time as hours and minutes separated by a point
12c (Me)	✓	4:05pm	**Calculate time intervals from clocks and timetables**
	error 3	4:45pm	subtracted time using 1hr=100min, suggesting times are decimal
13 (Ca)	✓	814	**Use efficient written methods to add and subtract integers**
14 (Ca)	✓	382	**Use efficient written methods to add and subtract integers**
	error 3	752	added instead of subtracted in a 3-digit vertical subtraction task
	error 4	422	took smaller digit from larger in a 3-digit vertical subtraction task
15 (Me)	✓	A and E	**Calculate the perimeter and area of rectilinear shapes**
	error 3	A and C, **or** D and E	confused *area* and *perimeter*
	error 4	C and D	counted diagonals as length of side in a perimeter task
16 (CN)	✓	−1	**Count from any given number in whole-number and decimal steps, extending beyond zero when counting backwards**
	error 3	3	miscounted when adding integers
	error 4	+1	misinterpreted the minus sign when adding integers
	error 5	9 or −9	added the numbers and combined the signs of integers separately when adding integers
17 (CN)	✓	6	**Solve simple problems involving direct proportion by scaling quantities up or down**
	error 3	48 **or** 96	ignored information in a missing-value ratio problem, suggesting a focus on 2 of the 3 numbers in the question
	error 4	8	made an additive error, suggesting preference for doubling or adding on in missing value ratio task
18a (Sh)	✓	B	**Estimate angles, ... in shapes**
	error 3	D	selected angle with smallest arms as smallest angle
	error 4	C	selected angle with smaller arms as smaller angle
18b (Sh)	✓	A and D	**Recognise that enlargements preserve angle**
	error 3	B,C **or** A, E **or** A, C **or** C, D	incorrectly identified angles that were not equal, suggesting 'size of angle' is conceived of as 'width between ends of arms'
19 (Ca)	✓	2.5, 25	**Use understanding of place value to multiply and divide whole numbers and decimals by 10, 100 or 1000**
	error 3	25, 250	wrote $0.25 \times 10 = 25$, suggesting place-value misconception

Question	Code	Response	Objective/Error Description
20 (CN)	✓	−3.5	**Understand negative numbers as positions on a number line**
	error 3	−4.25, −4.5 **or** −4.1	counted up from −4 to −4.25 or −4.5 or −4.1 on a scale, suggesting misconception of number line
21 (Ca)	✓	10	**Find fractions and percentages of whole-number quantities (e.g. 5/8 of 96, 65% of £260)**
	error 3	15	was partially correct in ratio task, but selected wrong value to multiply by
22a (CN)	✓	100	**Explain what each digit represents in whole numbers ... round ...these numbers**
	error 3	80	confused 'to the nearest 100' with 'to the nearest 10' in rounding task
22b (CN)	✓	1000	**Explain what each digit represents in whole numbers ... round ...these numbers**
	error 3	900	rounded down instead of up
	error 4	950	rounded 'to nearest 10' instead of 'to nearest 100'
23 (NF)	✓	41	**Use knowledge of multiplication facts to derive quickly squares of numbers to 12 × 12 and the corresponding squares of multiples of 10**
	error 3	9^2 **or** 81	calculated $4^2 + 5^2 = 81$, suggesting a commutability of adding and squaring
	error 4	18	calculated squares by doubling
24 (Ca)	✓	4 squares shaded	**Find fractions and percentages of whole-number quantities (e.g. 5/8 of 96, 65% of £260)**
	error 3	10 shaded	interpreted 10% as 10 parts, ignoring the % sign
25 (Me)	✓	from 145 inclusive up to, but not including, 155	**Appreciate that a measurement given to the nearest 10 may be inaccurate by up to 5 in either direction**
26 (CN)	✓	25, 73.32, 73.5, 73.65, 120	**Partition, round and order decimals with up to three places, and position them on the number line**
	error 3	73.65, 73.32, 73.5, 25, 120	ordered decimals smaller than wholes, e.g. 73.5 < 25, suggesting a conception of all decimals as parts less than one
	error 4	25, 120, 73.5, 73.32, 73.65	decimal point was treated as invisible/ignored in a decimal ordering task
	error 5	25, 73.5, 73.32, 73.65, 120	ordered wholes correctly but then 73.5 < 73.32, suggesting decimals are conceived as two values separated by a point
	error 6	73.5, 73.32, 73.65, 25, 120	ordered decimals as larger than wholes

Question	Code	Response	Objective/Error Description
27 (CN)	✓	⅛, ¼, ½, ⅝, ¾	**Order a set of fractions by converting them to fractions with a common denominator**
	error 3	½, ¼, ⅛, ¾, ⅝	ordered fractions by selecting unit fractions first, ½ < ¼ < ⅛ < ¾ < ⅝
	error 4	½, ¼, ¾, ⅛, ⅝	ordered fractions by denominator only, ignoring numerator
	error 5	⅝, ⅛, ¾, ¼, ½	correctly ordered fractions by denominators, but misused numerators
	error 6	⅛, ¼, ⅝, ½, ¾	incorrectly ordered ⅝ and ½ in otherwise correct fraction sequence
28 (NF)	✓	0.08	**Use knowledge of place value and multiplication facts to 10 × 10 to derive related multiplication and division facts involving decimals (e.g. 0.8 × 7, 4.8 ÷ 6)**
	error 3	0.8	wrote 0.2×0.4=0.8, suggesting decimals are treated as two numbers separated by a point
	error 4	0.6	read × as + in a calculation
29 (Ca)	✓	5/8	**Add and subtract simple fractions and those with common denominators**
	error 3	5/16	added denominators when adding fractions
	error 4	21	ignored fraction symbols in a fraction addition
30 (HD)	✓	E	**Use the language associated with probability to discuss events, including those with equally likely outcomes**
	error 3	A or C	selected choice of a spinner incorrectly, suggesting they are prone to the 'gambler's fallacy' (the mistaken notion that the odds for something with a fixed probability increase or decrease depending upon recent occurrences)
31 (Sh)	✓	A and C	**Visualise and draw on grids of different types where a shape will be after reflection, after translations, or after rotation through 90° or 180° about its centre or one of its vertices**
	error 3	A and D, **or** B and E	incorrectly modelled a word problem requiring rotation as a reflection
32 (Me)	✓	(−8, −2)	**Use conventions and notation for 2-D coordinates in all four quadrants**
	error 3	(−8, 2) or (2, −8)	incorrectly identified a negative coordinate as positive
	error 4	(−2,−8)	wrote x,y coordinates in wrong order
33 (Sh)	✓		**Visualise and draw on grids of different types where a shape will be after reflection**
34 (NF)	✓	1190	**Use knowledge of place value and multiplication facts to 10 × 10 to derive related multiplication and division facts involving decimals (e.g. 0.8 × 7, 4.8 ÷ 6)**
	error 3	1150	made carry error in vertical multiplication problem

Question	Code	Response	Objective/Error Description
35 (Sh)	✓	(7,9)	**Describe, identify and visualise parallel and perpendicular edges or faces; use these properties to classify 2-D shapes**
	error 3	(6,8) **or** (6,9)	made a counting or estimation error in identifying fourth coordinate of parallelogram
36 (Me)	✓	1.2m	**Select and use standard metric units of measure and convert between units using decimals to two places (e.g. change 2.75 litres to 2750 ml, or vice versa)**
	error 3	1020cm **or** 12m	wrote 1m + 20cm = 1020 or 12.0, suggesting 1000 or 10cm in a metre
	error 4	1.02m	wrote 1.02m suggesting 20cm was 0.02m

To find a pupil's **age-standardised score**, first calculate that pupil's chronological age in years and *completed* months. For example, a pupil born on 18 December 2000 who sat the test on 10 February 2010 has an age of 9 years and 1 month.

A separate conversion table is provided for each test, towards the end of this Manual. Each conversion table converts a raw score, shown vertically, into a standardised score, based on the pupil's chronological age, shown in the top row. For example, a pupil aged 9 years 11 months scoring 31 on **MaLT 9** has a standardised score of 107.

Pupils scoring very low or very high for their age – outside the score range provided in the conversion table – should be recorded as having a standardised score of 70– or 140+, respectively.

Having first obtained a pupil's standardised score, his or her **percentile score** can be read-off directly from Table 2.

The pupil's **National Curriculum level** and 'Mathematics Age' are derived from his or her total raw score on the test – refer to Tables 3 and 4, respectively.

If you are using the **Scorer/Profiler CD-ROM**, all of these performance measures are generated automatically. Additionally, the Scorer/Profiler enables you to produce a range of listings, reports and group performance statistics.

Guidance on what these various measures *mean* is given in the next section.

Age-standardised scores

There are a number of advantages to using age-standardised scores for measuring progress and comparing summative performance. These include:

■ They are standardised to an average score of 100, immediately showing whether a pupil is above or below average, compared to the reference sample.

■ They allow comparisons to take into account the pupils' ages, to the nearest completed month: older pupils are likely to have higher *raw* scores than younger pupils, but could have a lower *standardised* score. This allows pupils to be put in rank order of achievement after age has been accounted for.

■ They allow a pupil's scores from different standardised tests to be compared directly.

Standardised scores are especially helpful when exploring value-added, for it remains unfair on schools to be judged as poor if they have a very weak intake. Standardised scores enable the teacher to illustrate with confidence where the class or individual sits with respect to other pupils from across the country and from a complete range of schools.

For teachers wishing to use age-standardised scores, therefore, the main conversion tables allow you to derive standardised scores from pupils' raw scores, by month of chronological age.

Standardised scores are the most appropriate scores to use for most purposes. They provide important information on the extent to which pupils within each age group are performing compared with their age peers.

The standardised scores in Figure 1 range between 70 and 130, and the mean is 100. The six vertical bands determined by the standard deviation (SD) of 15, enable you to group pupils into:

■ those whose performance is within an age-appropriate range (within one SD either side of the mean: i.e. 85–115);

■ those who are well below or above average in this regard (between one and two SDs either side of the mean: i.e. 70–85 and 115–130);

■ those who are very weak or excellent for their age (between two and three SDs either side of the mean: *i.e.* below 70 or above 130).

Some caution is required when interpreting standardised scores at either end of the scale: results at the extremes are necessarily based on data from fewer pupils.

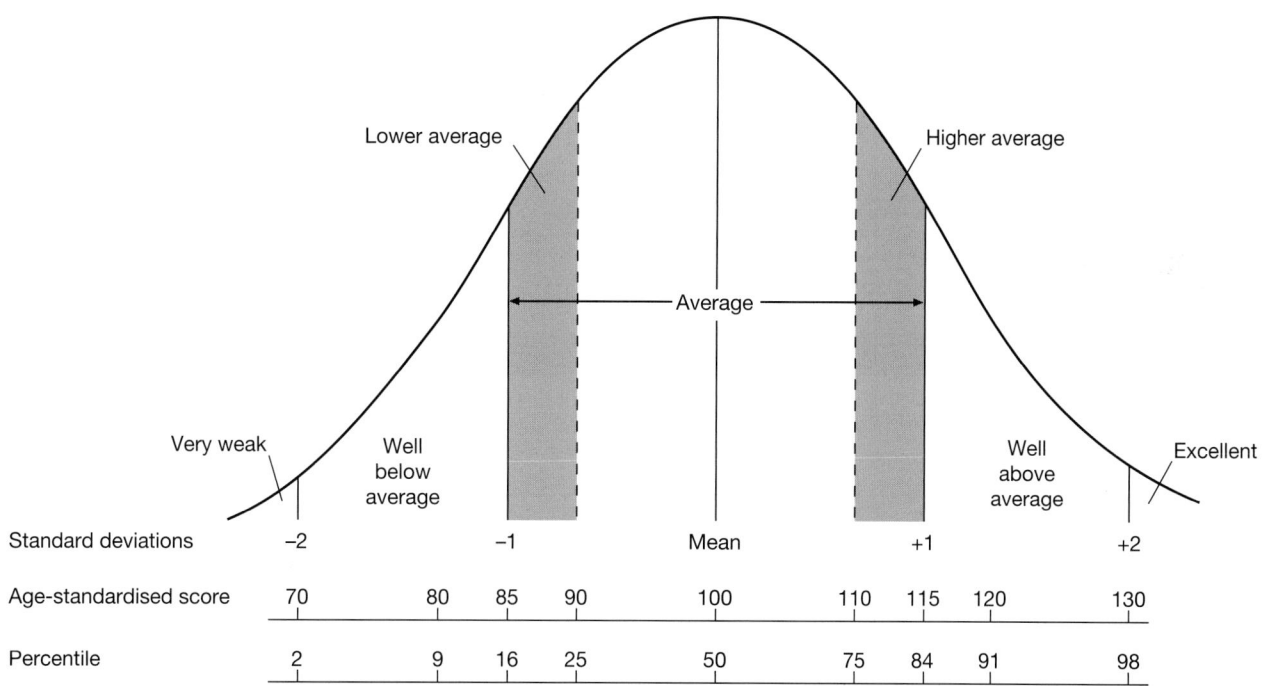

Standardised score	Qualitative interpretation of standardised scores	Standard deviation from mean	Percentile	Percentage of normal population
>130	Excellent	>+2	>98	2.27
116–130	Well above average	+1 to +2	84–98	13.59
110–115	*higher average*			
85–115	Average/age-appropriate	−1 to +1	16–83	68.26
85–90	*lower average*			
70–84	Well below average	−1 to −2	2–15	13.59
<69	Very weak	<−2	<2	2.27

Figure 1: Relationship between standardised test scores and qualitative interpretations

Percentile scores

Percentile scores give alternative information concerning a pupil's performance in comparison to his or her age group. They show the *percentage* of the group from whom norms were obtained, which scored *below* the pupil's standardised score. So a standardised score at the 68th percentile is comfortably within the average range, since it means that 68 per cent of the group scored below the pupil's standardised score. A standardised score at the 16th percentile, however, means that only 16 per cent had a lower result. Scores below the 16th percentile (i.e. two standard deviations below the mean) are of concern, as they indicate performance that is well below average.

Caution is needed when interpreting percentile scores, as they can be confused with percentages. Remember that a standardised score at the 68th percentile does *not* mean that the pupil responded correctly to 68 per cent of the items. It means that 68 per cent of the group from whom norms were obtained, scored below this pupil's standardised score.

Table 2: Percentile scores

Standardised Score	Percentile	Standardised Score	Percentile	Standardised Score	Percentile
139+	99+	109	72	89	24
133–8	99	108	70	88	22
130–2	98	107	68	87	20
128–9	97	106	66	86	18
126–7	96	105	63	85	16
125	95	104	60	84	14
123–4	94	103	58	83	13
122	93	102	55	82	12
121	92	101	52	81	11
120	91	100	50	80	9
119	90	99	48	79	8
118	89	98	45	78	7
117	87	97	42	76–7	6
116	86	96	40	75	5
115	84	95	37	73–4	4
114	82	94	34	71–2	3
113	80	93	32	70	2
112	78	92	30	70–	1
111	77	91	28		
110	74	90	26		

National Curriculum levels

Although age-standardised scores and percentiles can also be used to report progress, a disadvantage is that these may imply a spurious degree of precision and lead to an inappropriate emphasis on rank order. The alternative approach, using National Curriculum levels subdivided into three 'bands' of achievement, is probably fairer and gives more information than levels alone, but does not give undue emphasis to small differences in scores in the same manner that an age-related rank order may.

Table 3 enables you to convert raw scores into National Curriculum levels, and to subdivide each level into a, b and c, where:

a   is fully secure at the level

b   is comfortably at the level and

c   indicates performance just at the level;

This subdivision allows for more informative reporting to parents and pupils, and shows progress in finer increments than whole levels. Note, however, that progress from year to year is likely to be uneven.

Table 3 gives the mark range which equates to each National Curriculum level and sub-level appropriate to the **MaLT 8–11** tests.

Table 3: Test mark ranges and indicative National Curriculum sub-levels

MaLT 8

Range of test marks	Indicative National Curriculum sub-levels
–6	working towards 1a
7–9	1a
10–13	2c
14–18	2b
19–23	2a
24–28	3c
29–33	3b
34–38	3a
39+	4c or better

MaLT 9

Range of test marks	Indicative National Curriculum sub-levels
–4	working towards 2c
5–7	2c
8–11	2b
12–15	2a
16–20	3c
21–26	3b
27–31	3a
32+	4c or better

MaLT 10

Range of test marks	Indicative National Curriculum sub-levels
–9	working towards 3c
10–14	3c
15–19	3b
20–24	3a
25–29	4c
30–34	4b
35–38	4a
39+	4a or better

MaLT 11

Range of test marks	Indicative National Curriculum sub-levels
–7	working towards 3c
8–11	3c
12–16	3b
17–19	3a
20–23	4c
24–28	4b
29–32	4a
33+	5c or better

Mathematics ages

Some teachers and parents find it easier to appreciate a score if it is converted into the 'mathematics age' to which it corresponds (Table 4). This can be misleading, however, because mathematics attainment is not 'developmental' and is dependent on prior teaching.

The 'mathematics age' for a particular raw score is simply the age at which this score would be the average score of a national sample of children of that age. So a pupil with a 'mathematics age' of 9:3, whatever his or her chronological age, is performing at the level typical of average-ability pupils aged 9 years 3 months.

Table 4: Mathematics Ages

MaLT 8

Raw Score	Mathematics Age (years: months)	Raw Score	Mathematics Age (years: months)
1–11	below 6:7	24	8:4
12	6:7	25	8:6
13	6:9	26	8:8
14	6:11	27	8:9
15	7:1	28	8:10
16	7:3	29	9:1
17	7:5	30	9:3
18	7:6	31	9:4
19	7:8	32	9:6
20	7:10	33	9:8
21	7:11	34	9:11
22	8:1	35+	above 9:11
23	8:3		

MaLT 9

Raw Score	Mathematics Age (years: months)	Raw Score	Mathematics Age (years: months)
1–9	below 6:7	22	9:4
10	7:6	23	9:5
11	7:8	24	9:7
12	7:10	25	9:8
13	8:0	26	9:10
14	8:2	27	10:0
15	8:4	28	10:2
16	8:6	29	10:3
17	8:7	30	10:5
18	8:9	31	10:7
19	8:11	32	10:9
20	9:0	33	10:11
21	9:2	34+	above 10:11

MaLT 10

Raw Score	Mathematics Age (years: months)	Raw Score	Mathematics Age (years: months)
1–9	below 8:6	23	10:3
10	8:6	24	10:5
11	8:8	25	10:6
12	8:10	26	10:8
13	9:0	27	10:9
14	9:2	28	10:11
15	9:4	29	11:0
16	9:5	30	11:2
17	9:7	31	11:4
18	9:8	32	11:5
19	9:10	33	11:7
20	9:11	34	11:9
21	10:1	35	11:11
22	10:2	36+	above 11:11

MaLT 11

Raw Score	Mathematics Age (years: months)	Raw Score	Mathematics Age (years: months)
1–13	below 9:7	24	11:5
14	9:7	25	11:7
15	9:9	26	11:9
16	9:11	27	12:0
17	10:2	28	12:2
18	10:4	29	12:4
19	10:6	30	12:6
20	10:8	31	12:9
21	10:11	32	13:0
22	11:1	33+	above 13:0
23	11:3		

Progress and value-added

Pupil progress across school years can be determined by using the tables included in the manual. Consider, for example, Nita (aged 8:9) who scored 19 out of 45 on **MaLT 8** and, a year later (aged 9:9), now scores 22 out of 45 on **MaLT 9**.

Mathematics age

Using mathematics age to measure Nita's progress from **MaLT 8** to **MaLT 9**, looking up Table 4 for **MaLT 8** and **MaLT 9**, the difference is from 7:8 to 9:4 – about the same as 20 months of development. Nita has therefore progressed a further 8 months, in addition to her expected development over the last 12 months.

Scale score

The scale score can be used to compare performances between pupils, taking papers from different years, and hence to compare progress. The following table shows the number of **MaLT** scale score points within one level of the National Curriculum.

MaLT test	Scale scores in a NC level
5–7	11
8–11	10 or 9
12–14	8, 7 or 6

After **MaLT 7**, each NC level represents on average about two years' progress. From the scale score conversion table (pages 62–3), Nita's scale score has increased from 55 to 61. This is roughly equivalent to one level of the National Curriculum, and she can be said to have made substantially more than expected progress.

Age-standardised scores

To compare Nita's development with the norm, we use age-standardised scores. Using the conversion tables for **MaLT 8** and **MaLT 9** respectively:

■ Nita's raw score of 19 in **MaLT 8**, at age 8:9, gives an age-standardised score of 89.

■ Nita's raw score of 22 in **MaLT 9**, at age 9:9, gives an age-standardised score of 95.

Nita has clearly improved, as a pupil with a standardised score of 89 would not have been expected to score 22 on the **MaLT 9** test until age 10:4 (see the conversion table for **MaLT 9**: the age-standardised score for 22/45 at age 10:4 is 89). So Nita has progressed a total of 19 months – approximately 7 months more than the norm of 12 months.

Value-added

Strictly speaking, value-added (and so *average* value-added) should only be calculated using scale scores. Theoretically, the scale score is a linear scale, which means that these scores can be added, subtracted and averaged, whereas averaging raw and standardised scores is prone to giving errors (though often not much difference is found in practice).

For example, a teacher used the table on pages 62–3 to obtain each pupil's scale scores on **MaLT 8** and **MaLT 9**, taken a year apart, and found the class *average* scale score had increased from 55 to 60, giving an average value-added of 5 (corresponding to approximately half of one NC level at this age).

This class's average age had increased from 8:9 to 9:9, and this represents an average raw score increase from 19 (scale score of 55 on **MaLT 8**) to 20 (scale score of 60 on **MaLT 9**) and standardised score from 89 to 92. Thus the teacher can say that her class's added value was about 'as expected' for a group with this attainment range.

A similar calculation can be made using the appropriate column in the scale score conversion table if the same **MaLT** test given at the beginning of the year is repeated at the end of the year.

Caveats

There are several important caveats in measuring progress in these ways, and these must be borne in mind when interpreting such measurements.

First, the standard error in these measurements (especially for individuals) can be substantial (see Table 7). As a general rule, one can say that the expected error for a class average is about a fifth that of each individual. However, this may still be substantial.

Second, the implications of this for comparing value added from one year to the next (especially when that average is particularly high or low) may be problematic. This problem is often described as 'regression to the mean': a very high score one year is statistically more likely to be an error, and if this decreases the next year this may just be a 'regression to the mean' rather than a real deterioration (or vice versa).

It is vitally important to bear this in mind when providing evidence of a class's or an individual's progress: better to produce a series of results and look at trend rather than try to interpret a pair of results.

Error Analysis: diagnosing weaknesses and misconceptions

Diagnosing pupils' specific errors is at the heart of helping children to identify what they are doing wrong, why and what to do about it – i.e. to learn from their mistakes. Very often, specific errors in response to specific tasks, or patterns of responses to related tasks, are also indicative of the likely next stages in learning.

Identifying the patterns of errors common among a class of pupils can help target and plan significant teaching. It should be borne in mind when undertaking this form of analysis, however, that performance will naturally reflect recent teaching.

What are MaLT diagnostics?

We attempt to *diagnose* a child's mathematical misconception from their erroneous response to a question, rather as a doctor might diagnose an infection from the symptom of a high temperature.

For instance, when asked to *'Circle all the shapes that are one-quarter shaded'* (**MaLT 9**, Q27, shows a variety of regular and irregular shapes with numbers of parts shaded), 35% shaded shapes A (a quarter of a square) and C (a vertical strip of a circle, divided into four vertical strips of unequal area). It might be inferred that the many children who thought the circle was ¼ shaded had only a partial understanding of 'fractions' and simply interpreted the question as being about counting whole numbers of 'parts', not yet realising that it is essential that the 'parts' be equal.

Similarly with **MaLT 11**, Q26, when asked to put the numbers *73.32, 73.65, 25, 120, 73.5* in order, while 36% gave the right answer, some 41% mis-ordered the numbers with 18% ordering correctly except for saying that 73.32 is bigger than 73.5 It might be inferred that these children thought that because 5 is less than 32, 0.5 is less than 0.32, not yet realising that the digits *after* the decimal point represent progressively much smaller values. (In addition, 10% ordered all the numbers with a decimal part first, followed by 25 and 120, and 11% did the opposite. Note that a similar error was made by children taking **MaLT 10**.)

Each **MaLT** answer scheme has a code and description of each significant erroneous response found in our analysis of a national representative sample of over 1000 children. Answers were deemed 'significant' if (i) a significant number of children made the response, and (ii) the response was interpretable as a significant one educationally.

However, diagnosis is not a perfect art – further investigation and questioning may lead to a different inference about the child's thinking that leads to a particular response or error. One might infer that those 10% of children (see **MaLT 9**, Q34) who answered that ¾ has the same value as ⅔ might be using an additive strategy (add the same to the top number as the bottom number, so as to maintain the difference between the two). In fact, a few (only 3%) also chose ½, which might be selected for the same reasons. But it is possible that some of those who think ⅔ = ¾ are just picking the fraction they think is closest by some estimation procedure, or by thinking of fractions of a cake that would look the same, for example.

Or one might infer that the 19% that (see **MaLT 10**, Q17a) when asked to put the numbers in order: 143, 62.5, 47 from smallest to largest, wrote the whole numbers first: 47, 143, then 62.5, might simply be ignoring the decimal point, i.e. treating 62.5 as if it were 625, a common response by children at a very early stage in regard to decimal conceptions. In **MaLT 10**, Q17b, we found that 20% of children did the same thing with the five decimals given. However, it is possible that some of these children believe that decimals (in general) are larger than whole numbers. Only an interview or discussion can clarify the underlying conceptions definitively.

Sometimes a *sequence* of answers (correct and incorrect) can provide significant diagnostics for teaching: for example, while 84% correctly solved the missing addend *60 + ? = 100* (**MaLT 8**, Q3a), only 46% correctly solved **MaLT 8**, Q3b: *79 + ? = 100*. The difference is accounted for largely by pupils who made certain errors on Q3b, namely answering '20' or '30' (about 11%) and answering '31' (12%). Many of the others made no response.

Similarly, in **MaLT 11**, Q5, children are told that peanuts cost 70p for 100g, and are asked to *(a)* calculate the cost of 250g (57% correct), *(b)* calculate how much can be bought for £3.50 (49% correct), and *(c)* calculate the cost of 120g (18% correct). Clearly, the additional difficulty in part *(c)* arises from the harder fraction involved (adding on 1/5th) compared to whole numbers and halves in the other ratios, even though pupils had a calculator available for this question. Similarly in **MaLT 11**, Q12, the last part (13% correct) is much harder than the first two (81% and 64%) because of the additional difficulty of the calculation with subtracting time. Again consider the extra difficulty in **MaLT 11**, Q14, compared with **MaLT 11**, Q13: the subtraction calculation (68%) is somewhat harder than the addition (86%), at least when no calculator is available – the difference can be largely accounted for by those 12% who made the 'smaller from larger' error saying that *567 − 185 = 422*.

It may be that in a class of 30 children there will be groups who have reached quite different stages with topics such as these, and this can be important to teaching.

Why use MaLT diagnostics?

Diagnostic assessment is an important part of formative assessment, or 'Assessment for Learning' (AfL). It provides specific information on what children can and can't do, and what they think and believe. A teacher who is aware of the state of development of the thinking of an individual child or group of children can better plan their teaching – in the selection of tasks, the organisation of group work, and the development of class discussion.

In the above cases of representing fractions like ¼ or understanding decimals, groups at different stages might best be focussing on different tasks and discussions. Even then there will perhaps be some children who have gone beyond all these stages with fractions, or others who have not yet any concept of fraction. A teaching plan should in that case incorporate these differences.

But a class that has scored very highly on all the fraction or decimal questions should probably be moving on to other topics and might well be wasting time working on these topics.

The levels that **MaLT 8–11** assess are roughly indicated by the following tables that relate to the raw scores: children who score in the range indicated typically correctly answered questions assessing the targets indicated.

MaLT 8 raw score	Typically is able to...
Raw score > 9 *(approximately the level 2 boundary)*	... can add and subtract to 20, write down numbers in symbolic form 100s *(but perhaps not 1000s)* given in words, count down in 100s, and up in 10s through 100, eg solve missing addend *60 + ? = 100*, make simple pictograph interpretations, and shade a quarter as one part *(but perhaps not equivalent fractions)*
Raw score > 23 *(approximately the level 3 boundary)*	... can also find 'double 2-digit numbers' *(but not with breaking tens)*, write down numbers in symbolic form to 1000s, use multiples/counting in 3s, 5s, 10s 20s to solve problems, solve simple multiplication problems, recognise times tables, use 'symmetry' and recognise triangles, correctly add/subtract, both e.g. *79 + ? = 100* and horizontal subtraction of 2-digit numbers
Raw score >39 *(approximately level 4 boundary)*	... can also recognise representations for ¼, deal with place value to 100s and can count up/down in 70s, solve division problems including with money, aware of commutativity and distributivity, make more difficult pictograph interpretations of pictographs, read a scale/ruler/clock and solve problems with time, rotation of figures, and understands 'to the nearest 10'. *And may also:* ... represent division problems with division signs, solve division tasks with sets shown solve missing addend sums with 3 digits, recognise equivalent fractions for ½, and recognise 'right angles' in any orientation

MaLT 9 raw score	Typically is able to...
Raw score > 5 *(approximately the level 2 boundary)*	... can recognise parts of shapes, interpret bar graphs, count in 4s, understand place value (tens) and perform 2-digit subtraction.
Raw score > 16 *(approximately the level 3 boundary)*	... can also make more complex interpretations from a table/timetable/pictogram, understand multiplication and solve problems/number sentences involving multiplication and division, order the negative integers, reflect a shape in vertical line and understand the concept of hexagon.
Raw score > 31 *(approximately the level 4 boundary)*	... can also read a Venn Diagram, solve more difficult problems with charts and pictograms, read axes on graphs and scales on number lines (in 100s and 1000s), convert Kg to g, round to the nearest 10, find areas by counting squares/half-squares, recognise line symmetry and 180 degree rotation, read the coordinates of a point (though may make errors if the point lies on an axis), count up in 30s 'through the hundred' *(but perhaps not through the thousand)*, use a division sign and record £3.05 correctly *And may also:* ...count up 'through the thousand' in 10s, 30s, etc, subtract 3-digit numbers (algorithmic), identify some equivalent fractions, estimate the mass of an object, recognise 'right angles' in any orientation, and solve some harder problems involving charts, division, times-tables.

MaLT 10 raw score	Typically is able to...
Raw score > 2/3 *(approximately the level 2 boundary)*	... can read a scale involving divisions by 2s, and interpret a table of information, and convert kg to g *(but maybe not hard conversions g to kg)*
Raw score > 8/9 *(approximately the level 3 boundary)*	... can also make more complex interpretations from a table/timetable/ pictogram, understand multiplication and solve problems/number sentences involving multiplication and division, and 2-digit subtraction, place −15 on a thermometer, reflect a shape in a diagonal line and understand how to use a Venn Diagram
Raw score > 25 *(approximately the level 4 boundary)*	... can also identify equivalent fractions, complete number sentences and solve problems requiring knowledge of tables, money, % and addition with more than 3 digits, can order integers and count up in 0.2s, and easy sequences of harder numbers *(but not difficult cases with decimals)*, can solve simple ratio involving doubling, find the coordinates of a point, understands 'to the nearest 1000, and the concept of right angle and 90-degree rotation
Raw score > 37/8 *(approximately the level 5 boundary)*	...can also 3 digit subtraction, solve harder number sentences with fractions, multiplication, and calculations with hours and minutes, harder ratio (demanding breaking down and building-up strategy), correctly reading scales with intervals in 0.2, and understand nets *And may also:* ...interpret distance time graphs, calculate with addition of decimals (not all to the same number of places), perform harder metric conversions, and fractions of large numbers.

MaLT 11 raw score	Typically is able to...
Raw score > 8–9 *(approximately the level 3 boundary)*	... can read and use information from tables, perform 3-digit addition algorithm, round to the nearest 100, and perform simple calculations with money and partially understand angle size
Raw score > 18 *(approximately the level 4 boundary)*	... can also complete number sentences and solve problems requiring reading of tables and calculations with money and time *(but may still make decimal errors with time)*, perimeter, understands 'rounding', can perform 3-digit subtraction algorithm, can add negative integers, and has some understanding of chance
Raw score > 33 *(approximately the level 5 boundary)*	... can also solve harder problems involving arithmetic (including multiplication algorithm, single digit), money and ratio (e.g. demanding breaking down and building up strategy, rounding the answer up or down, subtracting times correctly, using squared notation, etc), understand decimal place-value and %, read negatives (e.g. coordinates and correctly reading scales with intervals in −0.5), and understand reflection (diagonal mirror) *And may also:* ...calculate average and range of data, manipulate fractions, including equivalence, understand and calculate perimeter and area, harder ratio and decimal calculations.

Using the diagnostic information

It is easy to say 'teaching should take account of assessment' but much more difficult to say *how*. AfL suggests the use of many *general* teaching strategies in the classroom (such as use of Traffic Lights, peer- and self-assessment, etc). The use of diagnostic assessment, however, is more *specific* and so each diagnosis may need to be related to the particular topic and stage of development. This suggests a particular 'local' plan of action.

For instance, in **MaLT 9**, Q21, many children misread the point of the scale as being 2.2 instead of 2.4, this is a very common error in scale reading, which involves counting each interval as 'one' (or sometimes as here one-tenth, in other cases one-hundred, etc) instead of working out the interval from the information given. A good local strategy for helping children in such cases is to ask them to count-on with their choice of interval until they reach the next labelled mark on the scale. This then may induce a feeling that they have gone wrong, and a reflection on how to find the right choice of interval. Other similar means are well known: checking symmetry by folding, equal ratios or fractions by working with a real context (pie/rectangle split into parts, etc).

There are several general teaching strategies that can be helpful, however. With individual children who have made an apparently significant error, the teacher/tutor can generally be advised to interview the child to ascertain what the thinking or misconception is behind a response, rather than simply correcting or taking the inference for granted without this investigation. It may even be that the child has found a perfectly intelligent answer that the mark scheme deemed 'wrong': if many children produce such 'incorrect' answers then the question may be suspect as a measure of attainment.

The articulation and discussion of the conceptions behind a response can be the focus of discussion with small groups and even whole classes. If groups of children work cooperatively, then one suggested teaching strategy is to have different groups discuss a variety of responses to a task and then have each group present to the whole class their preferred response and their arguments for it.

Very commonly, a class teacher may select children (or groups) to argue for a variety of responses, usually choosing the order of the children so that they argue from less sophisticated to more sophisticated choices, and the whole class benefits from the exposition and sees the progression of ideas.

For instance, in **MaLT 8**, when asked to subtract *37 − 18 = ?*, while 44% got the right answer, 8% answered 21 or 29 (suggesting the argument that you subtract the digits separately, or the error of failing to carry). A further 4% *added* to get 55, whist a further group made no coherent response.

Similarly in **MaLT 9**, when asked what number is ten less than 4000, while 31% got the right answer, 18% answered 3090 (suggesting the subtraction of ten from 100, but a bug in breaking through 100s and 1000s). A further 7.5% wrote 3000 and 9% wrote 3900. A further group made no coherent response.

In such cases a teacher might ask a class or group to discuss the reasons for these answers, even if they were made by only a few children in the class, and consider the pros and cons, before discussing other answers, so that the class hears the arguments and each child has the opportunity to formulate their argument and evaluate others. Needless to say, the teacher's own view is best left unvoiced while this discussion takes place, though most teachers will want to express their argument rather than have the wrong answer accepted by the class or group!

Sometimes arguments about a sequence of answers to related questions might be worth hearing out. For instance, we looked at several different questions relevant to understandings of fractions above.

Where such distinctions are found through **MaLT** assessment, then a teacher can adopt a strategy of making these differences explicit (e.g. by asking children with different responses to explain what they did for others) and encouraging evaluation of these differences in approaches or ideas by individuals, groups and with classes in peer and self-assessment.

Calculator vs non-calculator scores

As noted previously, the front cover of the **MaLT 11** test booklet provides spaces to record the 'calculator score' and 'non-calculator score'. These are an aid to record-keeping, however, and can *not* be used to compare calculator-mathematics and non-calculator-mathematics attainments. Although questions are easier with a calculator, not every question in the 'calculator' section absolutely requires one: if the pupil chooses *not* to use the calculator, calculations are obviously harder/take longer, but the pupil's response is then not related to calculator skill *per se*.

That said, if it is apparent from the class record sheet that pupils have made a disproportionate number of errors in the calculator section, this might suggest they need systematic practice in the use of the calculator.

The pupil 'performance map'

The Version 2 **MaLT Scorer/Profiler** can be used with *all* of the **MaLT** tests, and includes an 'overview' facility which allows you to monitor individual pupil performance across all ten tests – from Key Stage 1 to Key Stage 3.

For each test, the user-friendly **MaLT Scorer/Profiler** fully automates pupil age calculations and all raw-score conversions to standardised score, percentile, maths age (for **MaLT 5–11**) and National Curriculum level, as well as generating class and whole-yeargroup performance analyses and reports. You can also *mark* the pencil-and-paper tests directly on-screen, allowing you to easily capture pupils' errors as well as correct answers and enabling full diagnostic reporting – including a 'performance map' (Figure 2) as well as a range of achievement and error reports.

Every pupil has particular strengths and weaknesses that will show up in the performance map. When you examine the pupil's answers, you can check to see when there is a change from correct answers to incorrect answers, and at what level of demand this is occurring. Other reports look at attainment targets, and if there are marked differences between them this will alert you to significant extra achievement or where there is an area of the subject to be revisited. Equally, if the pattern is very patchy, you may wish to ask the pupil if there are parts of the subject which have been forgotten or have failed to be understood at the time.

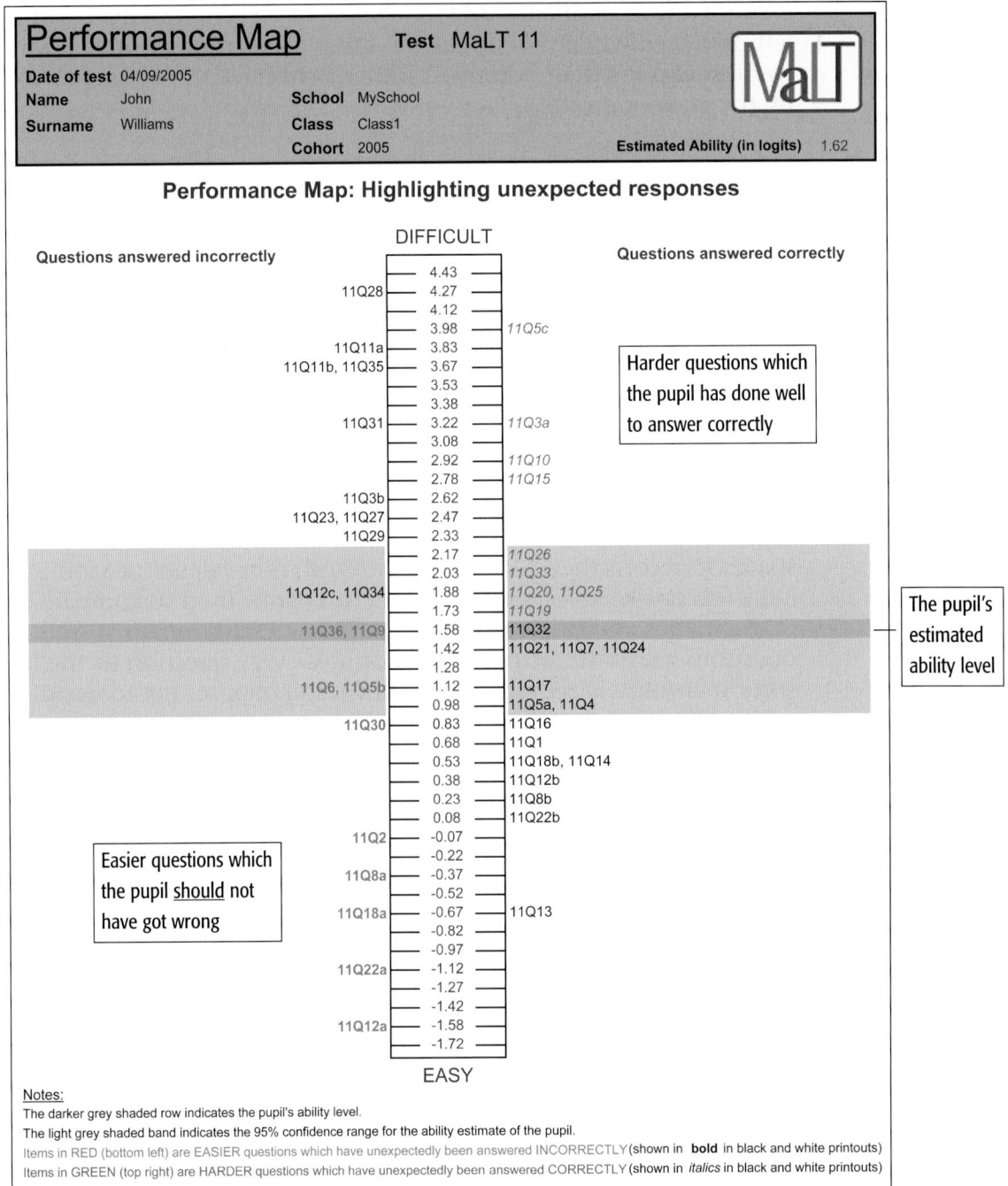

Figure 2

The Scorer/Profiler will also produce a class report to compare class performance on each item with the standardisation sample, highlighting those that are significantly easier/harder as well as average scores by attainment target and gender.

 **Test Development and Standardisation**

Item and test development

Items were written to the curriculum documents for the National Curriculum and National Numeracy Strategy for England and Wales. Each item was linked to a level and specification, and with anticipated conceptual or other errors, usually based on data from comparable items from previous research.

The pre-test took place in April 2004. It involved 2471 pupils aged 4–15 in 35 schools in England and Wales, comprised of a cross-section of schools and attainment structure (using teacher estimates of attainment) representative of population. The sample took two tests: a main paper, and a second 'calibration' or 'anchor' paper made up of questions that were either extra, replacement items (if needed) or from adjacent papers to enable us to estimate the difficulties of items on all of the tests on common scales.

Test refinement involved minor amendments, selecting items and balancing tests to provide curriculum and attainment coverage consistent with National Curriculum and other guidelines, but with few misfitting items.

The main standardisation test in February/March 2005 involved a nationally representative sample of 12591 pupils (minimum 1015 and maximum 1390 per year group) from 120 schools in England and Wales (Table 5). The sample was stratified by geography, school type/status and pupil attainment.

Table 5

MaLT	5	6	7	8	9	10	11	12	13	14
Male	496	669	752	710	666	685	671	599	552	590
Female	513	680	634	645	572	614	641	617	608	645
not known	6	8	4	3	0	1	0	6	1	3
Total	1015	1357	1390	1358	1238	1300	1312	1222	1161	1238

Test statistics and reliability

The mean, standard deviation and internal consistency of the test used in the main study are shown in Table 6.

Table 6

MaLT	5	6	7	8	9	10	11	12	13	14
Year	R	1	2	3	4	5	6	7	8	9
mean	18.1	16.7	15.8	20.8	20.7	19.65	22.6	18.5	17.6	16.7
s.d.	5.7	6.5	6.2	8.5	9.7	9.6	10.2	9.4	9.5	8.2
consistency	0.87	0.89	0.87	0.91	0.93	0.92	0.93	0.92	0.93	0.91

Equating scores via the scale score

The equation of test scores was achieved using the linked pre-test and main standardisation test dataset (excluding a few items that changed or were deemed flawed) using item response theory.

This allowed the creation of a common scale (called the 'scale score') to link the raw scores of the tests: test conversion between adjacent years can be carried out by converting both years' scores to the scale score, thus allowing value-added calculations.

Equating scores between different tests is relatively reliable and valid with adjacent years, or even within a Key Stage. But interpretations involving comparison over a number of years always needs to be sensitive to 'curriculum effects': pupils in later years are expected to perform at a given level over a wider curriculum in order to gain a particular 'scale score'. This problem can lead to invalid interpretations if a wide range of year groups are involved.

Cut scores

The National Curriculum levels were obtained from teacher estimates of pupil levels. By equipercentile equation over each year's test and over the three years encompassing each year's test (i.e. the test in question, and those for both the preceding and following years), estimates of cut scores for each relevant National Curriculum level were obtained. Weight was given to the cut values based on frequencies of estimates and our interpretation of where the level expertise would reside. Note that these teacher estimates were made in February, approximately half-way through the school year.

Age standardisation

Raw score to age-standardised score equations were calculated using deciles for each month made on (i) each year's data, (approximately 15 months' age difference, as measured in February from the year targeted) and smoothly extended by (ii) groups of three years' data encompassing each year (approximately 39 months' age difference as measured in February of the year targeted, or the year above/below). This age range was finally extended by a few months using a non-linear extrapolation.

The result is therefore a compromise between the effect of maturation within the year group (effective over the 15 months as at February 2005) and growth in attainment over the three school years. Reliability and validity of age standardisation is best with the middle 15 months of the conversion table, and due care is needed in interpreting extreme values and ages.

The standardised scale for each year is equated to an average of 100, and each standard deviation to 15.

Confidence intervals

All test scores are estimates which are subject to error – perhaps because a pupil is simply having an 'off' day. A pupil aged 8 years 11 months scoring 24 on **MaLT 9** has a standardised score of 107. To calculate a confidence interval for their standardised score, you have first to refer to Table 7 and then read off the minimum and maximum scores in the age-standardisation table too. For example, a raw score of 24 on **MaLT 9** has a min/max of 19/28, corresponding to min/max standardised scores of 100/112. This means we can be 90% confident that the pupil's true score lies within this range.

Table 7: 90% confidence limits

MaLT 8

Raw Score	min	max	Raw Score	min	max
1	0	4	23	18	27
2	1	5	24	19	28
3	1	6	25	20	29
4	2	7	26	21	30
5	3	9	27	22	31
6	3	10	28	23	31
7	4	11	29	24	32
8	5	12	30	25	33
9	6	13	31	26	34
10	6	14	32	27	35
11	7	15	33	28	36
12	8	16	34	29	37
13	9	17	35	30	38
14	10	18	36	31	39
15	11	19	37	32	40
16	12	20	38	33	41
17	13	21	39	34	41
18	14	22	40	36	42
19	14	23	41	37	43
20	15	24	42	38	44
21	16	25	43	40	44
22	17	26	44	41	45

MaLT 9

Raw Score	min	max	Raw Score	min	max
1	0	4	23	18	28
2	1	5	24	19	28
3	1	7	25	20	30
4	2	8	26	21	30
5	3	9	27	22	31
6	3	10	28	23	32
7	4	11	29	24	33
8	5	12	30	25	34
9	6	13	31	26	35
10	7	14	32	27	36
11	7	15	33	29	37
12	8	17	34	30	38
13	9	18	35	31	38
14	10	19	36	32	39
15	11	20	37	33	40
16	12	21	38	34	41
17	13	22	39	35	42
18	14	23	40	36	42
19	15	24	41	37	43
20	16	25	42	38	44
21	17	26	43	40	44
22	17	27	44	41	45

MaLT 10

Raw Score	min	max	Raw Score	min	max
1	0	4	23	18	28
2	1	6	24	19	29
3	1	7	25	20	29
4	2	8	26	21	30
5	3	9	27	22	31
6	3	10	28	23	32
7	4	11	29	24	33
8	5	12	30	25	34
9	6	13	31	26	35
10	6	14	32	27	36
11	7	16	33	28	37
12	8	17	34	29	38
13	9	18	35	31	39
14	10	19	36	32	39
15	11	20	37	33	40
16	12	21	38	34	41
17	13	22	39	35	42
18	14	23	40	36	42
19	15	24	41	37	43
20	15	25	42	38	44
21	16	26	43	40	44
22	17	27	44	41	45

MaLT 11

Raw Score	min	max	Raw Score	min	max
1	0	4	23	18	28
2	1	5	24	19	29
3	1	7	25	20	29
4	2	8	26	21	30
5	3	9	27	22	31
6	3	10	28	23	32
7	4	11	29	24	33
8	5	12	30	25	34
9	6	13	31	26	35
10	6	14	32	27	36
11	7	16	33	28	37
12	8	17	34	29	38
13	9	18	35	31	38
14	10	19	36	32	39
15	11	20	37	33	40
16	12	21	38	34	41
17	13	22	39	35	42
18	14	23	40	36	42
19	14	24	41	37	43
20	15	25	42	38	44
21	16	26	43	40	44
22	17	27	44	41	45

Conversion Tables

MaLT 8 conversion table: standardised scores

Age in years and completed months

Raw Score	7:0	7:1	7:2	7:3	7:4	7:5	7:6	7:7	7:8	7:9	7:10	7:11	8:0	8:1	8:2	
1																1
2																2
3	73	72	71	71	70	70										3
4	76	76	75	74	74	73	72	72	71	71	70					4
5	80	79	78	77	77	76	75	75	74	73	73	72	72	71	70	5
6	82	82	81	80	79	79	78	77	77	76	75	75	74	73	73	6
7	85	84	83	83	82	81	80	80	79	78	78	77	76	76	75	7
8	87	87	86	85	84	83	83	82	81	80	80	79	78	78	77	8
9	90	89	88	87	86	86	85	84	83	82	82	81	80	79	79	9
10	92	91	90	89	88	88	87	86	85	84	84	83	82	81	80	10
11	94	93	92	91	90	89	89	88	87	86	85	85	84	83	82	11
12	96	95	94	93	92	91	90	90	89	88	87	86	85	85	84	12
13	97	97	96	95	94	93	92	91	90	90	89	88	87	86	85	13
14	99	98	97	97	96	95	94	93	92	91	90	90	89	88	87	14
15	101	100	99	98	97	96	96	95	94	93	92	91	90	89	89	15
16	103	102	101	100	99	98	97	96	95	94	94	93	92	91	90	16
17	104	103	102	101	101	100	99	98	97	96	95	94	93	92	92	17
18	106	105	104	103	102	101	100	99	98	98	97	96	95	94	93	18
19	107	106	105	104	104	103	102	101	100	99	98	97	96	95	95	19
20	109	108	107	106	105	104	103	102	101	101	100	99	98	97	96	20
21	110	109	108	107	107	106	105	104	103	102	101	100	99	98	98	21
22	111	111	110	109	108	107	106	105	104	104	103	102	101	100	99	22
23	113	112	111	110	109	109	108	107	106	105	104	103	102	101	101	23
24	114	113	112	112	111	110	109	108	107	106	106	105	104	103	102	24
25	115	115	114	113	112	111	110	110	109	108	107	106	105	104	103	25
26	117	116	115	114	114	113	112	111	110	109	108	108	107	106	105	26
27	118	117	116	116	115	114	113	112	112	111	110	109	108	107	106	27
28	119	119	118	117	116	115	115	114	113	112	111	111	110	109	108	28
29	121	120	119	118	118	117	116	115	114	114	113	112	111	110	109	29
30	122	121	120	120	119	118	117	117	116	115	114	114	113	112	111	30
31	123	122	122	121	120	120	119	118	117	117	116	115	114	113	113	31
32	124	124	123	122	122	121	120	120	119	118	117	117	116	115	114	32
33	126	125	124	124	123	122	122	121	120	120	119	118	117	117	116	33
34	127	127	126	125	125	124	123	123	122	121	120	120	119	118	117	34
35	129	128	127	127	126	125	125	124	123	123	122	121	121	120	119	35
36	130	129	129	128	128	127	126	126	125	124	124	123	122	122	121	36
37	132	131	130	130	129	129	128	127	127	126	126	125	124	124	123	37
38	133	133	132	132	131	130	130	129	129	128	127	127	126	125	125	38
39	135	135	134	133	133	132	132	131	131	130	129	129	128	128	127	39
40	137	137	136	136	135	134	134	133	133	132	132	131	131	130	129	40
41	139	139	138	138	137	137	136	136	135	135	134	134	133	133	132	41
42					140	140	139	139	138	138	137	137	136	136	135	42
43													140	140	139	43
44																44
45																45
	7:0	7:1	7:2	7:3	7:4	7:5	7:6	7:7	7:8	7:9	7:10	7:11	8:0	8:1	8:2	

Age in years and completed months

	8:3	8:4	8:5	8:6	8:7	8:8	8:9	8:10	8:11	9:0	9:1	9:2	9:3	9:4	9:5	Raw Score
1																1
2																2
3									SCORE 70– IN THIS AREA							3
4																4
5	70															5
6	72	71	71	70	70											6
7	74	74	73	72	72	71	70	70								7
8	76	75	75	74	74	73	72	72	71	70	70					8
9	78	77	77	76	75	75	74	73	73	72	71	71	70	70		9
10	80	79	78	78	77	76	76	75	74	74	73	72	72	71	71	10
11	81	81	80	79	79	78	77	76	76	75	74	74	73	73	72	11
12	83	82	82	81	80	79	79	78	77	77	76	75	75	74	73	12
13	85	84	83	82	82	81	80	79	79	78	77	77	76	75	75	13
14	86	85	85	84	83	82	82	81	80	79	79	78	77	77	76	14
15	88	87	86	85	85	84	83	82	81	81	80	79	79	78	77	15
16	89	88	88	87	86	85	84	84	83	82	81	81	80	79	78	16
17	91	90	89	88	87	87	86	85	84	83	83	82	81	80	80	17
18	92	91	91	90	89	88	87	86	86	85	84	83	82	82	81	18
19	94	93	92	91	90	89	89	88	87	86	85	84	84	83	82	19
20	95	94	93	93	92	91	90	89	88	87	87	86	85	84	83	20
21	97	96	95	94	93	92	91	91	90	89	88	87	86	86	85	21
22	98	97	96	95	95	94	93	92	91	90	89	89	88	87	86	22
23	100	99	98	97	96	95	94	93	92	92	91	90	89	88	87	23
24	101	100	99	98	97	97	96	95	94	93	92	91	90	90	89	24
25	103	102	101	100	99	98	97	96	95	94	94	93	92	91	90	25
26	104	103	102	101	100	100	99	98	97	96	95	94	93	92	92	26
27	106	105	104	103	102	101	100	99	98	97	97	96	95	94	93	27
28	107	106	105	104	104	103	102	101	100	99	98	97	96	95	94	28
29	109	108	107	106	105	104	103	102	102	101	100	99	98	97	96	29
30	110	109	108	108	107	106	105	104	103	102	101	100	100	99	98	30
31	112	111	110	109	108	107	107	106	105	104	103	102	101	100	99	31
32	113	113	112	111	110	109	108	107	107	106	105	104	103	102	101	32
33	115	114	113	113	112	111	110	109	108	107	107	106	105	104	103	33
34	117	116	115	114	114	113	112	111	110	109	108	108	107	106	105	34
35	118	118	117	116	115	115	114	113	112	111	110	110	109	108	107	35
36	120	120	119	118	117	116	116	115	114	113	112	112	111	110	109	36
37	122	121	121	120	119	119	118	117	116	115	115	114	113	112	111	37
38	124	123	123	122	121	121	120	119	118	118	117	116	115	115	114	38
39	126	126	125	124	124	123	122	122	121	120	119	119	118	117	116	39
40	129	128	127	127	126	126	125	124	124	123	122	121	121	120	119	40
41	131	131	130	130	129	128	128	127	127	126	125	125	124	123	123	41
42	135	134	134	133	132	132	131	131	130	129	129	128	128	127	126	42
43	139	138	138	137	137	136	136	135	135	134	133	133	132	132	131	43
44											140	140	139	139	138	44
45																45
	8:3	8:4	8:5	8:6	8:7	8:8	8:9	8:10	8:11	9:0	9:1	9:2	9:3	9:4	9:5	

MaLT 9 conversion table: standardised scores

Age in years and completed months

Raw Score	8:0	8:1	8:2	8:3	8:4	8:5	8:6	8:7	8:8	8:9	8:10	8:11	9:0	9:1	9:2	Raw Score
1																1
2	70	70														2
3	75	74	74	73	72	72	71	71	70							3
4	79	78	77	77	76	75	75	74	73	73	72	72	71	70	70	4
5	82	81	81	80	79	78	78	77	76	76	75	74	74	73	73	5
6	85	84	83	83	82	81	80	80	79	78	78	77	76	76	75	6
7	87	87	86	85	84	84	83	82	81	81	80	79	78	78	77	7
8	90	89	88	87	87	86	85	84	84	83	82	81	81	80	79	8
9	92	91	90	90	89	88	87	86	86	85	84	83	83	82	81	9
10	94	93	93	92	91	90	89	88	88	87	86	85	84	84	83	10
11	96	95	94	94	93	92	91	90	89	89	88	87	86	85	85	11
12	98	97	96	95	95	94	93	92	91	90	89	89	88	87	86	12
13	100	99	98	97	96	95	95	94	93	92	91	90	90	89	88	13
14	102	101	100	99	98	97	96	95	95	94	93	92	91	90	89	14
15	103	102	101	101	100	99	98	97	96	95	94	94	93	92	91	15
16	105	104	103	102	101	100	100	99	98	97	96	95	94	93	93	16
17	106	105	105	104	103	102	101	100	99	98	98	97	96	95	94	17
18	108	107	106	105	104	104	103	102	101	100	99	98	97	96	96	18
19	109	108	108	107	106	105	104	103	102	101	101	100	99	98	97	19
20	111	110	109	108	107	106	106	105	104	103	102	101	100	99	99	20
21	112	111	110	110	109	108	107	106	105	104	103	103	102	101	100	21
22	113	113	112	111	110	109	108	108	107	106	105	104	103	102	101	22
23	115	114	113	112	111	111	110	109	108	107	106	105	105	104	103	23
24	116	115	114	114	113	112	111	110	109	109	108	107	106	105	104	24
25	117	116	116	115	114	113	112	112	111	110	109	108	107	107	106	25
26	118	118	117	116	115	115	114	113	112	111	111	110	109	108	107	26
27	120	119	118	117	117	116	115	114	114	113	112	111	110	109	109	27
28	121	120	119	119	118	117	116	116	115	114	113	112	112	111	110	28
29	122	121	121	120	119	118	118	117	116	115	115	114	113	112	111	29
30	123	123	122	121	120	120	119	118	118	117	116	115	115	114	113	30
31	124	124	123	122	122	121	120	120	119	118	117	117	116	115	114	31
32	126	125	124	124	123	122	122	121	120	120	119	118	117	117	116	32
33	127	126	126	125	124	124	123	122	122	121	120	120	119	118	117	33
34	128	128	127	126	126	125	125	124	123	123	122	121	120	120	119	34
35	130	129	128	128	127	127	126	125	125	124	123	123	122	121	121	35
36	131	130	130	129	129	128	128	127	126	126	125	124	124	123	122	36
37	133	132	131	131	130	130	129	129	128	127	127	126	125	125	124	37
38	134	134	133	133	132	131	131	130	130	129	128	128	127	127	126	38
39	136	135	135	134	134	133	133	132	132	131	130	130	129	129	128	39
40	138	137	137	136	136	135	135	134	134	133	133	132	131	131	130	40
41	140	140	139	139	138	138	137	137	136	136	135	134	134	133	133	41
42						140	140	139	139	138	138	137	137	136	136	42
43														140	140	43
44																44
45																45

| | 8:0 | 8:1 | 8:2 | 8:3 | 8:4 | 8:5 | 8:6 | 8:7 | 8:8 | 8:9 | 8:10 | 8:11 | 9:0 | 9:1 | 9:2 | |

Age in years and completed months

Raw Score	9:3	9:4	9:5	9:6	9:7	9:8	9:9	9:10	9:11	10:0	10:1	10:2	10:3	10:4	10:5	Raw Score
1																1
2																2
3																3
4																4
5	72	71	71	70	70											5
6	74	74	73	72	72	71	71	70								6
7	76	76	75	74	74	73	73	72	71	71	70	70				7
8	78	78	77	76	76	75	74	74	73	73	72	71	71	70	70	8
9	80	80	79	78	78	77	76	76	75	74	74	73	72	72	71	9
10	82	81	81	80	79	79	78	77	76	76	75	75	74	73	73	10
11	84	83	82	82	81	80	79	79	78	77	77	76	75	75	74	11
12	85	85	84	83	82	82	81	80	79	79	78	77	77	76	75	12
13	87	86	85	85	84	83	82	82	81	80	80	79	78	77	77	13
14	89	88	87	86	85	85	84	83	82	82	81	80	79	79	78	14
15	90	89	89	88	87	86	85	85	84	83	82	82	81	80	79	15
16	92	91	90	89	88	88	87	86	85	84	84	83	82	81	81	16
17	93	92	92	91	90	89	88	87	87	86	85	84	83	83	82	17
18	95	94	93	92	91	90	90	89	88	87	86	86	85	84	83	18
19	96	95	94	94	93	92	91	90	89	88	88	87	86	85	85	19
20	98	97	96	95	94	93	92	92	91	90	89	88	87	87	86	20
21	99	98	97	96	96	95	94	93	92	91	90	90	89	88	87	21
22	101	100	99	98	97	96	95	94	93	93	92	91	90	89	88	22
23	102	101	100	99	98	98	97	96	95	94	93	92	91	91	90	23
24	103	103	102	101	100	99	98	97	96	95	95	94	93	92	91	24
25	105	104	103	102	101	100	100	99	98	97	96	95	94	93	93	25
26	106	105	105	104	103	102	101	100	99	98	97	97	96	95	94	26
27	108	107	106	105	104	103	102	102	101	100	99	98	97	96	95	27
28	109	108	107	107	106	105	104	103	102	101	100	100	99	98	97	28
29	111	110	109	108	107	106	106	105	104	103	102	101	100	99	98	29
30	112	111	110	110	109	108	107	106	105	104	104	103	102	101	100	30
31	114	113	112	111	110	110	109	108	107	106	105	104	103	103	102	31
32	115	114	114	113	112	111	110	109	109	108	107	106	105	104	103	32
33	117	116	115	114	114	113	112	111	110	109	109	108	107	106	105	33
34	118	118	117	116	115	114	114	113	112	111	110	110	109	108	107	34
35	120	119	118	118	117	116	115	115	114	113	112	112	111	110	109	35
36	122	121	120	120	119	118	117	117	116	115	114	113	113	112	111	36
37	123	123	122	121	121	120	119	119	118	117	116	116	115	114	113	37
38	125	125	124	123	123	122	121	121	120	119	119	118	117	116	116	38
39	127	127	126	126	125	124	124	123	122	122	121	120	119	119	118	39
40	130	129	129	128	127	127	126	125	125	124	123	123	122	121	121	40
41	132	132	131	131	130	129	129	128	128	127	126	126	125	125	124	41
42	135	135	134	134	133	133	132	132	131	130	130	129	129	128	127	42
43	139	139	138	138	137	137	136	136	135	135	134	134	133	133	132	43
44												140	140	139	139	44
45																45

SCORE 70– IN THIS AREA

Age in years and completed months

Raw Score	9:0	9:1	9:2	9:3	9:4	9:5	9:6	9:7	9:8	9:9	9:10	9:11	10:0	10:1	10:2	
1																1
2	72	71	71	70												2
3	76	76	75	74	74	73	72	72	71	71	70					3
4	80	79	79	78	77	77	76	75	74	74	73	72	72	71	71	4
5	83	82	82	81	80	79	79	78	77	77	76	75	74	74	73	5
6	86	85	84	84	83	82	81	80	80	79	78	77	77	76	75	6
7	89	88	87	86	85	84	83	83	82	81	80	80	79	78	77	7
8	91	90	89	88	87	86	86	85	84	83	82	82	81	80	79	8
9	93	92	91	90	89	88	88	87	86	85	84	83	83	82	81	9
10	95	94	93	92	91	90	89	89	88	87	86	85	84	84	83	10
11	97	96	95	94	93	92	91	90	89	89	88	87	86	85	84	11
12	98	98	97	96	95	94	93	92	91	90	89	88	88	87	86	12
13	100	99	98	97	96	95	95	94	93	92	91	90	89	88	87	13
14	102	101	100	99	98	97	96	95	94	93	92	92	91	90	89	14
15	103	102	101	100	100	99	98	97	96	95	94	93	92	91	90	15
16	105	104	103	102	101	100	99	98	97	96	95	95	94	93	92	16
17	106	105	104	103	102	102	101	100	99	98	97	96	95	94	93	17
18	108	107	106	105	104	103	102	101	100	99	98	97	96	95	95	18
19	109	108	107	106	105	104	103	102	102	101	100	99	98	97	96	19
20	110	109	108	107	107	106	105	104	103	102	101	100	99	98	97	20
21	111	111	110	109	108	107	106	105	104	103	102	101	101	100	99	21
22	113	112	111	110	109	108	107	106	106	105	104	103	102	101	100	22
23	114	113	112	111	110	110	109	108	107	106	105	104	103	102	101	23
24	115	114	113	113	112	111	110	109	108	107	106	105	105	104	103	24
25	116	115	115	114	113	112	111	110	109	109	108	107	106	105	104	25
26	117	117	116	115	114	113	112	112	111	110	109	108	107	106	105	26
27	119	118	117	116	115	115	114	113	112	111	110	109	109	108	107	27
28	120	119	118	117	117	116	115	114	113	112	112	111	110	109	108	28
29	121	120	119	119	118	117	116	115	115	114	113	112	111	110	109	29
30	122	121	121	120	119	118	118	117	116	115	114	113	113	112	111	30
31	123	123	122	121	120	120	119	118	117	116	116	115	114	113	112	31
32	124	124	123	122	122	121	120	119	119	118	117	116	115	115	114	32
33	126	125	124	124	123	122	121	121	120	119	118	118	117	116	115	33
34	127	126	126	125	124	124	123	122	121	121	120	119	118	118	117	34
35	128	128	127	126	126	125	124	124	123	122	121	121	120	119	118	35
36	130	129	128	128	127	126	126	125	124	124	123	122	121	121	120	36
37	131	130	130	129	129	128	127	127	126	125	125	124	123	122	122	37
38	133	132	131	131	130	130	129	128	128	127	126	126	125	124	124	38
39	134	134	133	132	132	131	131	130	129	129	128	128	127	126	126	39
40	136	135	135	134	134	133	133	132	131	131	130	130	129	128	128	40
41	138	138	137	137	136	135	135	134	134	133	133	132	132	131	130	41
42		140	140	139	139	138	138	137	137	136	136	135	134	134	133	42
43									140	140	139	139	138	138	137	43
44																44
45																45

	9:0	9:1	9:2	9:3	9:4	9:5	9:6	9:7	9:8	9:9	9:10	9:11	10:0	10:1	10:2

SCORE 70–
IN THIS AREA

10:3	10:4	10:5	10:6	10:7	10:8	10:9	10:10	10:11	11:0	11:1	11:2	11:3	11:4	11:5	Raw Score
															1
															2
															3
70															4
72	72	71	71	70											5
75	74	73	73	72	71	71	70	70							6
77	76	75	75	74	73	73	72	71	71	70	70				7
79	78	77	76	76	75	74	74	73	72	72	71	70	70		8
80	80	79	78	77	77	76	75	75	74	73	73	72	71	71	9
82	81	80	80	79	78	77	77	76	75	75	74	73	73	72	10
84	83	82	81	80	80	79	78	77	77	76	75	75	74	73	11
85	84	83	83	82	81	80	80	79	78	77	77	76	75	75	12
87	86	85	84	83	83	82	81	80	79	79	78	77	77	76	13
88	87	86	86	85	84	83	82	82	81	80	79	79	78	77	14
89	89	88	87	86	85	84	84	83	82	81	80	80	79	78	15
91	90	89	88	87	87	86	85	84	83	82	82	81	80	79	16
92	91	90	90	89	88	87	86	85	85	84	83	82	81	81	17
94	93	92	91	90	89	88	87	87	86	85	84	83	83	82	18
95	94	93	92	91	90	90	89	88	87	86	85	85	84	83	19
96	95	95	94	93	92	91	90	89	88	87	87	86	85	84	20
98	97	96	95	94	93	92	91	90	90	89	88	87	86	85	21
99	98	97	96	95	94	94	93	92	91	90	89	88	87	86	22
100	99	99	98	97	96	95	94	93	92	91	90	89	89	88	23
102	101	100	99	98	97	96	95	94	93	92	92	91	90	89	24
103	102	101	100	99	98	97	97	96	95	94	93	92	91	90	25
104	104	103	102	101	100	99	98	97	96	95	94	93	92	92	26
106	105	104	103	102	101	100	99	98	97	97	96	95	94	93	27
107	106	105	104	104	103	102	101	100	99	98	97	96	95	94	28
109	108	107	106	105	104	103	102	101	100	99	98	97	97	96	29
110	109	108	107	106	105	105	104	103	102	101	100	99	98	97	30
111	111	110	109	108	107	106	105	104	103	102	101	101	100	99	31
113	112	111	110	109	109	108	107	106	105	104	103	102	101	100	32
114	114	113	112	111	110	109	108	107	107	106	105	104	103	102	33
116	115	114	113	113	112	111	110	109	108	107	106	106	105	104	34
118	117	116	115	114	113	113	112	111	110	109	108	107	106	106	35
119	118	118	117	116	115	114	114	113	112	111	110	109	108	107	36
121	120	119	119	118	117	116	116	115	114	113	112	111	110	110	37
123	122	121	121	120	119	118	118	117	116	115	114	114	113	112	38
125	124	124	123	122	121	121	120	119	118	118	117	116	115	114	39
127	126	126	125	124	124	123	122	122	121	120	119	119	118	117	40
130	129	128	128	127	126	126	125	124	124	123	122	122	121	120	41
133	132	132	131	130	130	129	128	128	127	127	126	125	124	124	42
137	136	135	135	134	134	133	133	132	131	131	130	130	129	128	43
				140	140	139	139	138	138	137	137	136	136	135	44
															45
10:3	10:4	10:5	10:6	10:7	10:8	10:9	10:10	10:11	11:0	11:1	11:2	11:3	11:4	11:5	

Age in years and completed months

Raw Score	10:0	10:1	10:2	10:3	10:4	10:5	10:6	10:7	10:8	10:9	10:10	10:11	11:0	11:1	11:2	
1																1
2																2
3	73	72	72	71	71	70	70	70								3
4	76	76	75	75	74	74	73	73	72	72	71	71	71	70	70	4
5	79	78	78	77	77	76	76	75	75	75	74	74	73	73	72	5
6	81	81	80	80	79	79	78	78	77	77	76	76	76	75	75	6
7	84	83	83	82	82	81	81	80	80	79	79	78	78	77	77	7
8	86	85	85	84	84	83	83	82	82	81	81	80	79	79	78	8
9	88	87	87	86	86	85	85	84	83	83	82	82	81	81	80	9
10	90	89	89	88	87	87	86	86	85	85	84	84	83	82	82	10
11	92	91	90	90	89	89	88	87	87	86	86	85	85	84	84	11
12	93	93	92	92	91	90	90	89	89	88	87	87	86	86	85	12
13	95	94	94	93	93	92	91	91	90	90	89	88	88	87	87	13
14	97	96	95	95	94	93	93	92	92	91	90	90	89	89	88	14
15	98	98	97	96	96	95	94	94	93	93	92	91	91	90	90	15
16	100	99	98	98	97	97	96	95	95	94	93	93	92	92	91	16
17	101	100	100	99	99	98	97	97	96	95	95	94	94	93	92	17
18	103	102	101	101	100	99	99	98	97	97	96	96	95	94	94	18
19	104	103	103	102	101	101	100	100	99	98	98	97	96	96	95	19
20	105	105	104	103	103	102	102	101	100	100	99	98	98	97	96	20
21	107	106	105	105	104	104	103	102	102	101	100	100	99	98	98	21
22	108	107	107	106	106	105	104	104	103	102	102	101	100	100	99	22
23	109	109	108	107	107	106	106	105	104	104	103	102	102	101	101	23
24	111	110	109	109	108	108	107	106	106	105	104	104	103	103	102	24
25	112	111	111	110	109	109	108	108	107	106	106	105	105	104	103	25
26	113	113	112	111	111	110	110	109	108	108	107	107	106	105	105	26
27	114	114	113	113	112	111	111	110	110	109	108	108	107	107	106	27
28	116	115	114	114	113	113	112	112	111	110	110	109	109	108	107	28
29	117	116	116	115	115	114	114	113	112	112	111	111	110	109	109	29
30	118	118	117	117	116	115	115	114	114	113	113	112	111	111	110	30
31	119	119	118	118	117	117	116	116	115	115	114	113	113	112	112	31
32	121	120	120	119	119	118	118	117	117	116	115	115	114	114	113	32
33	122	122	121	121	120	120	119	118	118	117	117	116	116	115	115	33
34	123	123	122	122	121	121	120	120	119	119	118	118	117	117	116	34
35	125	124	124	123	123	122	122	121	121	120	120	119	119	118	118	35
36	126	126	125	125	124	124	124	123	123	122	122	121	121	120	120	36
37	128	127	127	127	126	126	125	125	124	124	123	123	122	122	121	37
38	129	129	129	128	128	127	127	126	126	126	125	125	124	124	123	38
39	131	131	130	130	130	129	129	128	128	128	127	127	126	126	125	39
40	133	133	132	132	132	131	131	130	130	130	129	129	128	128	128	40
41	136	135	135	134	134	134	133	133	132	132	132	131	131	130	130	41
42	138	138	138	137	137	136	136	136	135	135	135	134	134	133	133	42
43					140	140	140	139	139	139	139	138	138	138	137	137	43
44																44
45																45

	10:0	10:1	10:2	10:3	10:4	10:5	10:6	10:7	10:8	10:9	10:10	10:11	11:0	11:1	11:2

Raw Score	11:3	11:4	11:5	11:6	11:7	11:8	11:9	11:10	11:11	12:0	12:1	12:2	12:3	12:4	12:5
1															
2															
3															
4															
5	72	71	71	71	70	70									
6	74	74	73	73	72	72	71	71	71	70	70				
7	76	76	75	75	74	74	73	73	73	72	72	71	71	70	70
8	78	78	77	77	76	76	75	75	74	74	73	73	72	72	72
9	80	79	79	78	78	77	77	76	76	75	75	74	74	74	73
10	81	81	80	80	79	79	78	78	77	77	76	76	75	75	75
11	83	82	82	81	81	80	80	79	79	78	78	77	77	76	76
12	85	84	83	83	82	82	81	81	80	80	79	79	78	78	77
13	86	85	85	84	84	83	83	82	82	81	81	80	80	79	79
14	88	87	86	86	85	85	84	84	83	83	82	81	81	80	80
15	89	88	88	87	87	86	85	85	84	84	83	83	82	82	81
16	90	90	89	89	88	87	87	86	86	85	85	84	83	83	82
17	92	91	91	90	89	89	88	88	87	86	86	85	85	84	84
18	93	93	92	91	91	90	90	89	88	88	87	87	86	85	85
19	95	94	93	93	92	91	91	90	90	89	88	88	87	87	86
20	96	95	95	94	93	93	92	92	91	90	90	89	89	88	87
21	97	97	96	95	95	94	93	93	92	92	91	90	90	89	89
22	99	98	97	97	96	95	95	94	94	93	92	92	91	91	90
23	100	99	99	98	97	97	96	96	95	94	94	93	92	92	91
24	101	101	100	99	99	98	98	97	96	96	95	94	94	93	93
25	103	102	101	101	100	100	99	98	98	97	96	96	95	94	94
26	104	103	103	102	102	101	100	100	99	98	98	97	96	96	95
27	105	105	104	104	103	102	102	101	100	100	99	99	98	97	97
28	107	106	106	105	104	104	103	102	102	101	101	100	99	99	98
29	108	108	107	106	106	105	105	104	103	103	102	101	101	100	99
30	110	109	108	108	107	107	106	105	105	104	104	103	102	102	101
31	111	111	110	109	109	108	108	107	106	106	105	104	104	103	103
32	113	112	111	111	110	110	109	108	108	107	107	106	105	105	104
33	114	114	113	112	112	111	111	110	109	109	108	108	107	106	106
34	116	115	115	114	113	113	112	112	111	111	110	109	109	108	108
35	117	117	116	116	115	115	114	113	113	112	112	111	111	110	109
36	119	119	118	117	117	116	116	115	115	114	114	113	112	112	111
37	121	120	120	119	119	118	118	117	117	116	116	115	114	114	113
38	123	122	122	121	121	120	120	119	119	118	118	117	117	116	115
39	125	124	124	123	123	122	122	121	121	120	120	119	119	118	118
40	127	127	126	126	125	125	124	124	123	123	122	122	121	121	120
41	130	129	129	128	128	128	127	127	126	126	125	125	124	124	123
42	133	132	132	132	131	131	130	130	129	129	129	128	128	127	127
43	137	136	136	136	135	135	134	134	134	133	133	132	132	132	131
44								140	140	140	140	139	139	138	138
45															

SCORE 70– IN THIS AREA

Conversion table: raw score to scale score

Scale score	MaLT 5 (max. 30)	MaLT 6 (max. 30)	MaLT 7 (max. 30)	MaLT 8 (max. 45)	MaLT 9 (max. 45)	MaLT 10 (max. 45)	MaLT 11 (max. 45)	MaLT 12 (max. 45)	MaLT 13 (max. 45)	MaLT 14 (max. 45)
100										44
99									44	–
98									–	–
97									–	–
96								44	–	43
95								–	43	–
94								–	–	–
93								–	–	42
92								43	42	–
91							44	–	–	41
90							–	–	41	40
89							–	42	–	–
88						44	–	–	40	39
87						–	43	41	39	38
86						–	–	40	38	37
85					44	43	42	–	37	36
84					–	–	–	39	36	35
83				44	–	–	41	38	35	34
82				–	–	42	40	37	34	32
81				–	43	–	–	35	33	31
80				–	–	41	39	34	32	30
79				43	42	40	38	33	30	28
78				–	–	39	37	31	29	27
77				–	41	38	35	30	27	25
76				42	40	37	33	28	26	23
75				–	–	36	34	27	24	22
74				41	39	35	32	25	23	20
73				–	38	33	30	23	21	19
72			29	40	37	32	29	22	20	17
71			–	39	36	31	27	20	18	16
70			–	–	35	30	26	19	17	14
69			–	38	33	28	24	17	15	13
68			28	37	32	26	22	16	14	12
67			–	36	31	25	21	14	13	11
66			–	35	29	23	19	13	11	9
65			27	33	28	22	17	12	10	8
64		29	–	32	26	20	16	11	9	7
63		–	26	31	25	18	14	9	8	–
62		–	–	29	23	17	13	8	7	6
61		–	25	28	22	15	12	–	6	5
60		28	24	27	20	14	10	7	–	–
59		–	23	25	18	12	9	6	5	4
58		–	–	24	17	11	8	5	4	3
57		27	22	22	15	10	7	–	–	–
56		–	21	21	14	9	6	4	3	–
55	29	26	20	19	13	8	–	–	–	2

Scale score	MaLT 5 (max. 30)	MaLT 6 (max. 30)	MaLT 7 (max. 30)	MaLT 8 (max. 45)	MaLT 9 (max. 45)	MaLT 10 (max. 45)	MaLT 11 (max. 45)	MaLT 12 (max. 45)	MaLT 13 (max. 45)	MaLT 14 (max. 45)
54	–	–	19	18	11	7	5	3	2	–
53	–	25	18	17	10	6	4	–	–	–
52	–	24	17	15	9	5	–	2	–	–
51	28	23	16	14	8	4	3	–	–	1
50	–	–	14	13	7	–	–	–	1	
49	–	22	13	12	6	3	2	–		
48	27	21	12	11	5	–	–	1		
47	–	20	11	10	–	2	–			
46	26	19	10	9	4	–	–			
45	–	18	9	8	–	–	1			
44	25	17	8	7	3	–				
43	24	16	7	6	–	1				
42	–	15	–	5	2					
41	23	14	6	–	–					
40	22	13	5	4	–					
39	–	12	–	–	–					
38	21	11	4	3	1					
37	20	10	–	–						
36	19	9	3	2						
35	18	8	–	–						
34	17	–	2	–						
33	16	7	–	–						
32	15	6	–	1						
31	14	5	–							
30	13	–	–							
29	12	4	1							
28	11	–								
27	–	3								
26	10	–								
25	9	–								
24	8	2								
23	7	–								
22	6	–								
21	–	–								
20	5	1								
19	4									
18	–									
17	3									
16	–									
15	–									
14	2									
13	–									
12										
11	–									
10	1									

Class Record Sheet – MaLT 8

Pupil	1a	1b	2	3a	3b	4a	4b	5	6	7a	7b	8	9a	9b	10	11	12	13a	13b	14
1																				
2																				
3																				
4																				
5																				
6																				
7																				
8																				
9																				
10																				
11																				
12																				
13																				
14																				
15																				
16																				
17																				
18																				
19																				
20																				
21																				
22																				
23																				
24																				
25																				
26																				
27																				
28																				
29																				
30																				
31																				
32																				
33																				
34																				
35																				
Total of correct answers																				
Percentage correct																				
National percentage correct	89	91	86	84	46	81	39	66	32	91	77	65	72	71	26	19	61	69	50	33
NC level	2	3	3	3	3	3	3	3	3	2	2	3	2	2	3	3	3	3	3	3
Strand	CN	CN	CN	NF	NF	CN	CN	CN	CN	Ca	Ca	Ca	Me	Me	CN	Me	NF	NF	NF	Ca
Attainment Target	2	2	2	2	2	2	2	2	2	2	2	2	2	2	2	3	2	2	2	2
Question number	1a	1b	2	3a	3b	4a	4b	5	6	7a	7b	8	9a	9b	10	11	12	13a	13b	14

Attainment Target: **AT2** Number; **AT3** Shape, Space & Measures; **AT4** Data Handling

Strand: **CN** Counting & Understanding Number; **NF** Knowing & Using Number Facts; **Ca** Calculating;
      Sh Understanding Shape; **Me** Measuring; **HD** Handling Data

15	16	17a	17b	17c	18	19	20	21a	21b	22	23	24	25	26	27	28	29	30	31	32a	32b	33a	33b	34	Raw Score	SS
28	25	33	22	85	23	7	19	23	24	44	32	56	59	8	15	22	17	25	47	57	1	80	51	28		
3	3	3	3	3	3	3	3	3	3	3	4	3	3	3	3	3	3	2	3	2	2	3	3	3		
Sh	Me	HD	HD	HD	CN	CN	Ca	NF	NF	Ca	Me	Me	Sh	Ca	Ca	CN	Ca	Me	NF	Sh	Sh	CN	CN	Ca		
3	3	4	4	4	2	2	2	2	2	2	3	3	3	2	2	2	2	3	2	3	3	2	2	2		
15	16	17a	17b	17c	18	19	20	21a	21b	22	23	24	25	26	27	28	29	30	31	32a	32b	33a	33b	34		

SS: Standardised Score (from the conversion table).

Class Record Sheet – MaLT 9

Pupil	1	2	3	4a	4b	5	6	7a	7b	8	9	10	11	12	13	14a	14b	15	16	17a
1																				
2																				
3																				
4																				
5																				
6																				
7																				
8																				
9																				
10																				
11																				
12																				
13																				
14																				
15																				
16																				
17																				
18																				
19																				
20																				
21																				
22																				
23																				
24																				
25																				
26																				
27																				
28																				
29																				
30																				
31																				
32																				
33																				
34																				
35																				
Total of correct answers																				
Percentage correct																				
National percentage correct	86	87	75	73	57	18	47	79	50	39	45	20	17	48	60	62	21	72	52	92
NC level	2	2	3	3	3	2	3	3	3	4	4	4	4	4	4	4	4	3	4	3
Strand	CN	HD	NF	Me	Me	Sh	CN	HD	HD	CN	Me	Me	Me	HD	Sh	NF	NF	HD	CN	Sh
Attainment Target	2	4	2	4	4	3	2	4	4	2	2	3	4	4	3	2	2	4	2	3
Question number	1	2	3	4a	4b	5	6	7a	7b	8	9	10	11	12	13	14a	14b	15	16	17a

Attainment Target: **AT2** Number; **AT3** Shape, Space & Measures; **AT4** Data Handling

Strand: **CN** Counting & Understanding Number; **NF** Knowing & Using Number Facts; **Ca** Calculating;
   Sh Understanding Shape; **Me** Measuring; **HD** Handling Data

17b	18	19	20	21	22	23	24a	24b	25	26	27	28	29	30	31	32	33a	33b	34	35	36	37	38a	38b	Raw Score	SS
43	70	68	47	10	44	39	37	20	66	30	3	53	44	31	48	51	40	28	15	10	25	62	50	32		
3	2	3	3	4	4	3	3	4	4	3	3	3	3	3	3	5	3	3	3	4	4	4	4	4		
Sh	CN	CN	CN	Me	Me	Ca	HD	HD	CN	Ca	CN	NF	NF	Ca	Sh	Me	CN	CN	CN	NF	Me	Sh	Sh	Sh		
3	2	3	2	3	3	2	4	4	2	2	2	2	2	2	3	3	2	2	2	2	3	3	3	3		
17b	18	19	20	21	22	23	24a	24b	25	26	27	28	29	30	31	32	33a	33b	34	35	36	37	38a	38b		

SS: Standardised Score (from the conversion table).

MaLT photocopy master published by Hodder Education

Class Record Sheet – MaLT 10

Pupil	1a	1b	2	3a	3b	4	5a	5b	6a	6b	7	8a	8b	9	10a	10b	11	12	13	14
1																				
2																				
3																				
4																				
5																				
6																				
7																				
8																				
9																				
10																				
11																				
12																				
13																				
14																				
15																				
16																				
17																				
18																				
19																				
20																				
21																				
22																				
23																				
24																				
25																				
26																				
27																				
28																				
29																				
30																				
31																				
32																				
33																				
34																				
35																				
Total of correct answers																				
Percentage correct																				
National percentage correct	74	77	83	59	41	28	40	31	80	7	34	57	37	36	62	24	64	22	57	50
NC level	3	3	3	4	4	3	4	4	5	5	4	3	3	4	5	5	3	4	3	4
Strand	Ca	Ca	Me	CN	CN	Me	Ca	Ca	Me	Me	Me	Ca	Ca	CN	CN	CN	HD	Sh	HD	Ca
Attainment Target	2	2	2	2	2	3	2	2	3	3	3	2	2	2	2	2	4	3	4	2
Question number	1a	1b	2	3a	3b	4	5a	5b	6a	6b	7	8a	8b	9	10a	10b	11	12	13	14

Attainment Target: **AT2** Number; **AT3** Shape, Space & Measures; **AT4** Data Handling
Strand: **CN** Counting & Understanding Number; **NF** Knowing & Using Number Facts; **Ca** Calculating;
　　　Sh Understanding Shape; **Me** Measuring; **HD** Handling Data

15	16a	16b	17a	17b	18	19	20	21	22a	22b	23	24a	24b	25	26	27	28a	28b	29	30a	30b	31	32a	32b	Raw Score	SS
64	82	34	62	18	20	15	74	53	47	47	52	25	24	56	52	16	52	41	41	16	17	69	19	6		
3	3	3	4	5	4	5	4	4	4	4	4	3	4	4	3	4	3	3	4	4	4	4	4	4		
Me	HD	HD	CN	CN	Me	Ca	HD	Sh	CN	CN	CN	Ca	Ca	Sh	Sh	Sh	NF	NF	CN	Ca	Ca	Sh	HD	HD		
2	4	4	2	2	3	2	4	3	2	2	2	2	2	3	3	3	2	2	2	2	2	3	3	3		
15	16a	16b	17a	17b	18	19	20	21	22a	22b	23	24a	24b	25	26	27	28a	28b	29	30a	30b	31	32a	32b		

SS: Standardised Score (from the conversion table).

MaLT photocopy master published by Hodder Education

Class Record Sheet – MaLT 11

Pupil	1	2	3a	3b	4	5a	5b	5c	6	7	8a	8b	9	10	11a	11b	12a	12b	12c	13	14
									Calculator section												
1																					
2																					
3																					
4																					
5																					
6																					
7																					
8																					
9																					
10																					
11																					
12																					
13																					
14																					
15																					
16																					
17																					
18																					
19																					
20																					
21																					
22																					
23																					
24																					
25																					
26																					
27																					
28																					
29																					
30																					
31																					
32																					
33																					
34																					
35																					
Total of correct answers																					
Percentage correct																					
National percentage correct	63	74	21	29	63	57	49	18	63	61	83	77	45	18	24	19	81	64	40	86	68
NC level	4	4	3	3	4	5	5	5	4	4	3	3	3	5	5	4	3	4	4	3	3
Strand	NF	Ca	Ca	Ca	Ca	CN	CN	CN	Ca	Sh	HD	HD	Ca	Me	HD	HD	HD	Me	Me	Ca	Ca
Attainment Target	2	2	2	2	2	2	2	2	2	3	4	4	2	3	4	4	4	4	4	2	2
Question number	1	2	3a	3b	4	5a	5b	5c	6	7	8a	8b	9	10	11a	11b	12a	12b	12c	13	14

Attainment Target: **AT2** Number; **AT3** Shape, Space & Measures; **AT4** Data Handling

Strand: **CN** Counting & Understanding Number; **NF** Knowing & Using Number Facts; **Ca** Calculating;
Sh Understanding Shape; **Me** Measuring; **HD** Handling Data

15	16	17	18a	18b	19	20	21	22a	22b	23	24	25	26	27	28	29	30	31	32	33	34	35	36	Raw Score	SS
												Non-calculator section													

15	16	17	18a	18b	19	20	21	22a	22b	23	24	25	26	27	28	29	30	31	32	33	34	35	36
34	66	52	83	66	54	44	52	88	73	36	51	57	36	31	9	33	68	19	49	47	43	12	53
4	5	5	4	4	5	4	5	4	4	4	5	5	4	5	5	5	5	5	5	5	5	4	5
Me	CN	CN	Sh	Sh	Ca	CN	Ca	CN	CN	NF	Ca	Me	CN	CN	NF	Ca	HD	Sh	Me	Sh	NF	Sh	Me
3	2	2	3	3	2	2	2	2	2	2	2	2	2	2	2	2	4	3	2	3	2	2	3
15	16	17	18a	18b	19	20	21	22a	22b	23	24	25	26	27	28	29	30	31	32	33	34	35	36

SS: Standardised Score (from the conversion table).

MaLT photocopy master published by Hodder Education